Keep Showing Up

A Utah Pastor's Journey

Scott McKinney

Edited by Vince Font
www.glassspiderpublishing.com

Cover design by Judith S. Design & Creativity
www.judithsdesign.com

There are so many people I want to thank that have meant so much to us through the years. I do want to express my appreciation for Dave Holcomb, whose generosity has made this whole project possible. Beyond that, my great fear in naming names is that I will leave some people out. I will simply say that we are so grateful for all of the wonderful people God has brought into our lives.

I do want to say something about a special group of people. My kids had no idea what we were getting them into when we moved to Utah in 1989. They adapted amazingly well and have grown up to be difference-makers in this place. I want to thank them and their spouses: Ginny and Aaron, Annie and Nolan, Rob and Karli, Christy and Jon. I am so grateful for their friendship and the grandkids they have given us. What a blessing!

In our family, there is one person who has held it all together. It is my wife, Sara. She has held this family together with her love. She is my best friend and my partner in life and in this ministry. I am dedicating this book to her. The following words are apropos of Sara. "Her children arise and call her blessed; her husband also, and he praises her: Many women do noble things, but you surpass them all." (Proverbs 31:28-29)

Contents

Introduction 13

PART I: Our Story 19

Chapter 1: "All-American Family" 21

Chapter 2: "Anything But a Pastor" 25

Chapter 3: Going to Utah 29

Chapter 4: "You Have No Idea" 34

Chapter 5: Giants in the Land 40

Chapter 6: "It Will Never Happen Here" 44

Chapter 7: Life Happens 49

Chapter 8: Chapter Two 53

Chapter 9: Building a Home 57

Chapter 10: Junior Varsity Christianity? 61

Chapter 11: No Competition 66

Chapter 12: Less is More 70

PART II: Understanding Mormon Culture 77

Chapter 13: Cult or Culture? 79

Chapter 14: A Persecuted People 82

Chapter 15: From the Margins to the Mainstream 87

Chapter 16: Living with Tension 91

Chapter 17: "We're Christians Too!" 99

Chapter 18: "I Hope They Send Me on a Mission" 107

Chapter 19: "Families are Forever" 113

Chapter 20: Leaving Mormonism 117

PART III: What Would Jesus Do? 125

Chapter 21: The Challenges are Real 127

Chapter 22: A New Perspective 131

Chapter 23: Show Up 136

Chapter 24: Settle Down 140

Chapter 25: Reach Out 144

Chapter 26: Good News 150

Chapter 27: The Heart of the Matter 155

Chapter 28: Answering the Golden Questions 159

Chapter 29: "How We Know" 165

Chapter 30: Real Authority 170

Chapter 31: The Reason We Believe 177

Chapter 32: The One True Church 183

Chapter 33: The God We Worship 192

Chapter 34: God in Three Persons 198

Chapter 35: Pork Chop Theology 204

Chapter 36: Lift Up Your Eyes 210

Afterword 214

About the Author 216

Introduction

In 1996, several years after we moved to Utah, I was in John Wayne Airport in Southern California, waiting for my luggage. I found myself standing alone next to Rick Majerus, the men's basketball coach at the University of Utah. Majerus might have been one of the most well-known residents of Utah during the 90s. The Utes were having an amazing run, and Majerus was, to put it mildly, a character. He had a way of "telling it like it is."

Our bags took a long time arriving, and we ended up in a conversation. I wanted to talk about the Ute basketball program, but Majerus didn't seem interested in talking about himself. He wanted to know about me. He asked what I did for a living. I told him I was the pastor of a church just a few miles away from Brigham Young University (the Utes' archrival).

He looked at me and said, "Tough gig."

Coach Majerus made that statement from the perspective of being an outsider in this unique Utah culture we both lived in.

Thinking back on that conversation, I can certainly say that it *has* been a tough gig. What has made this a tough gig is that the church I have been the pastor of since 1989, CenterPoint Church, is located at the center point of Utah Valley. Utah Valley is in the middle of a unique and vastly influential religious culture. This valley is dominated in every way by the Church of Jesus Christ of Latter-day Saints.

The story of the LDS Church's dominance over this area begins in 1847 when Mormon pioneers led by Brigham Young arrived in the Salt Lake Valley. Brigham Young saw Utah as a place "The Saints" would be free to practice their religion without interference from the federal government. Very quickly, Brigham sent pioneers to settle the various valleys in the state. One of the first valleys to be settled was Utah Valley, directly south of Salt Lake Valley.

To Mormons, Utah is Zion. You see it in a lot of small ways. As you drive through the state, there are cities and places like Moroni, Nephi, and Lehi, all named after Book of Mormon characters. Utah is dominated by the LDS Church, not just religiously but politically, culturally, and financially.

Today, the LDS Church has grown to be an international church. The leadership of the church understands the importance of Utah to its overall mission.

Apostle Russell Ballard in 2015 said, "In one sense, the Church in Utah is the heart of the worldwide Church body. The heart is a muscle that pumps blood through the blood vessels of the circulatory system, providing the body with needed oxygen and nutrients. The Saints in Utah help pump gospel truths through the entire world—giving the members important spiritual oxygen and essential nutrients." (*LDS Living*, Sept. 16, 2015).

Even so, Utah is changing. There are demographic changes. Salt Lake City, which is where the LDS Church is headquartered, is a city of fewer than 200,000 and is now less than 20 percent LDS. Salt Lake County is now slightly below 50 percent Mormon. The Ogden area, home to Hill Air Force Base (AFB), has a large non-Mormon population. Park City is a place people move to for its mountain lifestyle and does not have even close to an LDS majority. In all these places, you cannot assume that people are LDS.

Utah County (which comprises all of Utah Valley) is different. The population of Utah County is over 600,000 people. An article in the July 16, 2017, edition of the *Salt Lake Tribune* was entitled "Salt Lake County is becoming less Mormon—Utah County is headed in the other direction."

The article reports that Utah County has risen from 83.6 percent LDS in 2009 to 84.7 percent in 2016.

CenterPoint Church is located in Orem on the I-15 freeway just south of the University Parkway exit, the busiest offramp in the valley. We are half a mile south of Utah Valley University, the largest university in the state with nearly 40,000 students. Most of these students are from Utah Valley and are overwhelmingly LDS. We are less than four miles from BYU. Of the 34,000 students at BYU, over 99 percent are Latter-day Saints. We are less than five miles from the Missionary Training Center where LDS missionaries are trained to go on missions all over the world. Not all Mormons live here. Almost all Mormons have ties here.

The practical effect of that is that in Utah County, people just assume that "everyone is Mormon." You overhear conversations as you stand in line in the grocery store where people talk of "primary," "relief society," "young men's," "young women's," and who is being called to be the next bishop. There is talk about sons and daughters being called to serve a mission and who is getting married in the temple. "The Church" seems to be a part of the air we breathe and the water we drink.

CenterPoint Church exists to reach people that live here at the center point of Mormon culture. That is what makes this a tough gig. It is also what makes it an exciting opportunity. We are an evangelical church. We are here because we have good news for these people. The good news is that salvation is by faith alone, in Christ alone, and we know that from the Bible alone. We believe that the news about Jesus is such good news that we want to share it with our neighbors.

The challenge of this place is that we are trying to communicate the gospel to people that believe in a different gospel. Mormons call their gospel "The Restored Gospel." We are trying to reach people that are aggressively trying to reach people like us. How do we do that? That is the question I hope to address in this book.

If you are one of our neighbors and a member of the Church of Jesus Christ of Latter-day Saints, I understand that there will be some things in this book that will be difficult to read. I would ask that you read the whole book. My hope is that it will be clear by the end that I love the people of Utah Valley and am grateful for the privilege to live my life here among some wonderful people.

Please understand, though, that I am not writing this for Latter-day Saints. I am writing this first and foremost for the people of CenterPoint Church. I am writing at a time when I have been the pastor of this church for more than 30 years. In the coming years, there is going to be a necessary transition for CenterPoint where I will no longer be the lead pastor of this church. There are some important things I want to pass on to this next generation of leaders.

I am also writing for other church leaders in Utah, hoping that some of what we have learned over the years will be helpful in their local churches. As I offer these insights, I do so with care. So often, as pastors talk about their ministries, you get the impression they have discovered something brand new that no one else in the history of the church has ever thought of.

Maybe they have, but I don't think it works that way. I do not have all of the answers. Churches in Utah, and the people that lead them, do face some unique pressures. The wisdom I have to offer as we face these situations has often been gained the hard way. I have made lots of mistakes. A lot of what I write is personal and comes from my own experience. I have also learned many things from other pastors, and I hope to continue to learn.

As we begin, let me set some expectations. If you are looking for a book that gives you ammo to help you win arguments with Mormons, this book will probably disappoint you. You will also be disappointed if you are looking for a book that minimizes the theological issues that exist between evangelicals and Mormons. The differences between what LDS and evangelicals believe are vast. What I do hope to do is equip people to be able to talk about faith issues with their LDS neighbors in a way that bears fruit.

I want to be an encouragement to the church in Utah, but I have also come to realize that some of the lessons we have learned in Utah might be helpful to churches elsewhere. When we moved here in 1989, we quickly realized that we needed to learn how to be a church in a place where (to use a sports analogy) we did not have the "home field advantage." We were playing away from home.

Something has happened to the church in America in the past generation, in our relationship with American culture at large. We have lost the home-field advantage. In many quarters, people no longer see the church as the solution to our problems, but as the problem itself. In Utah, we know something of what it is like to play away from home. Perhaps the local church in Utah has learned some lessons that will be helpful to other churches in other places where the culture is not cheering us on.

Over the last generation, I have talked to pastors of churches around the country. I have heard the same frustration on multiple occasions. Local church leaders will look at the mission and vision statements of the churches they lead and resonate with them. At the same time, there is the sense that the real (and unstated) mission of their church is to "do church" a little better than other churches in their area so they can get Christian consumers to decide to come and join them.

One thing that has happened here at CenterPoint Church over the years is that we have a sense of clarity as to why we exist. We do not exist to reach people in our area that have an evangelical Christian background (or that go to other evangelical churches). A church that seeks to do that in our valley will not last long. We are a church that exists to reach the people of this valley. We believe that what we are doing matters. It matters so much that it has kept us showing up through the years.

I am excited about the future of the local church in the state of Utah. I am encouraged by the unity that exists with those that are involved in this work. My hope is that our story would be a help to these churches and their leaders.

PART I:
Our Story

Chapter 1
"All-American Family"

In most places in America, people are not all that interested when you tell them that you are a pastor. In Utah, there are times I feel like the proverbial unicorn. The reason for this is that the LDS Church does not have pastors. LDS congregations are led by "bishops" who are called to their positions as unpaid volunteers.

When I meet people here in Utah and they find out I am a pastor, there is a natural curiosity followed by several questions. People will ask, "What is your real job?" "What is it like being a pastor around all of these Mormons?" "Were you sent here?"

People want to know if I come from a Mormon background. They want to know how I got here. Here is my story.

I was the youngest of four boys in what would have to be described as an all-American family. I had great parents. My mom and dad loved us. My dad was a lieutenant colonel in the Air Force. His stated goal in raising us was that he wanted to raise us to be good citizens. Part of being a good citizen was going to church. We were Presbyterians, and every Sunday we attended the local Presbyterian church.

My high school years were spent in a place called Rialto, California, 60 miles east of Los Angeles. The 60s and 70s were the era of "sex, drugs, rock and roll, and rebellion." In one sense, my brothers and I missed the

60s. For example, one way kids my age expressed that rebellion was guys wearing long hair. My dad was big on haircuts. Every other Saturday morning, he would take us out to Norton AFB to be shorn by Air Force barbers because, in my dad's words, "Those guys know how to cut hair."

We said, "Yes, sir," and went along with it because we loved our dad. My parents were strict. They stopped drinking and smoking as we grew up because they did not want us to do those things. My mom and dad were a lot of fun and created a home and a family that I was grateful to be a part of. In retrospect, we looked a lot like the perfect Mormon family.

My dad was my hero. He was the starting tailback for the LSU Tigers back before World War II. He then joined the Army Air Corps and flew fighters in China during the war. I wanted to make him happy. He wanted us to play football, and he also encouraged us toward military careers. He was pretty specific in what he wanted us to do. He wanted us to play football and go to a military academy.

For a while, things were going that way. My oldest brother, Bob, played football and graduated from the Air Force Academy. My brother Bill did the same at the Naval Academy. When I graduated from high school, my brother Keith was already at the Naval Academy. My high school grades were unspectacular, but I was recruited to play football and received an appointment to the Naval Academy in Annapolis, Maryland.

As one friend put it, going to the Naval Academy gives you an opportunity to fall in love with the Navy. I didn't. After being at the academy for a few months, I realized I had no desire to be in the Navy. I was completely uninterested in receiving a Naval education filled with classes like Naval Science and Engineering and Weapons. When I informed my dad that I wanted to leave and come home, he was not happy. There was incredible family pressure to stay. The thought of disappointing my dad was painful to me. I also did not want to look like a failure.

The problem was that, in many ways, I *was* a failure. I was not only failing academically but I had also missed much of my freshman football season with a separated shoulder. I was in constant trouble militarily. I reached a point of crisis. I was empty. I had no purpose.

It all came to a head when my brother Keith, who had similar issues, left the Academy at midyear. Keith was a committed Christian and had taken me on as his project. He was really all that I had to lean on. After he was gone, I had nothing left.

The night Keith left, I got alone in one of the classrooms at the Academy and told the Lord that if he wanted my life, he could have it. He took my sin, my shame, my guilt, and gave me his life. There is no other way to describe it; I was born again. I knew that I was loved and accepted by the God of the Universe because of Jesus. I came alive.

From that point on, my life changed. I had a sense of purpose. I had this great desire to serve God. I did not have any idea where that would take me, but I did know that it did not include the Navy. I decided to finish my Plebe year to prove to my dad that I wasn't leaving because it was too hard.

There was no way around it. My dad was deeply disappointed in me. I am so grateful for the way that God healed my relationship with my dad over the years. It took some time. This is where I feel I can relate to people that are leaving Mormonism. I felt that in leaving the Naval Academy, I was leaving the family faith and disappointing the expectations of my family. As I returned home, the world had changed for me.

I not only had a father who was deeply disappointed with me, but I also had a high school girlfriend who was a Latter-day Saint. None of our religious differences mattered before I went to the Academy. When I returned home, we began to discuss my newfound faith and, all of a sudden, those differences became a mountain between us. I began to read about the LDS Church. I could see there were huge differences between the LDS Church and biblical Christianity.

Maybe the biggest point of contention in our discussions had to do with the nature of God. Mormons believe in eternal progression: The idea is that God had once been a man, and that we can progress to become gods ourselves. On one occasion, I quoted Isaiah 43:10 to her. "Before me, no god was formed, nor will there be one after me."

At this, she said, "Okay, you are right. We are wrong."

"So what are you going to do?" I asked.

Her answer was, "Nothing. What you don't realize is that this is my family. These are my people. This is who I am."

The reality was that she did not believe I was right and she was wrong. All she was saying was that if all you have is the Bible, what I was saying made sense.

In her mind, Mormons had so much more. They had more scripture, a living prophet, and a restored priesthood. I realized then that being a Mormon was so much more than believing a set of theological truths. It was an entire way of life. We realized this was not going to work and decided to go our separate ways.

I graduated from Cal State San Bernardino with a degree in history. I had no clear direction in my life. I was open to almost anything. I decided to go to seminary because I wanted to learn, and I wanted to be prepared to do whatever God called me to do.

Chapter 2
"Anything But a Pastor"

The one thing I was not open to was becoming a pastor. My reasons were probably pretty shallow. I saw pastors as a seriously uptight group of people. I have a sense of humor. My time at the Naval Academy had also contributed to a tendency to question authority. It was not in me to do things just because everyone else was doing them.

In addition to all of that, I had an experience directly after graduating from college that confirmed I was not cut out to be a pastor. I went down to Louisiana, where I got a job as a deckhand on a tugboat from my uncle, the superintendent of a river construction company.

I learned a lot about life on that river. One Sunday, I wandered into a church in a small town called Simmesport, on the Red River. It was the Sunday school hour, and as I walked in, a man who seemed to be in charge immediately asked me to open in prayer. I said okay, and I prayed.

I must have done okay, because after that he told me the Sunday school teacher had failed to show and asked me if I would be willing to fill in and teach. He handed me a booklet, and I saw that the lesson was on Genesis 3. I had been doing some reading on that passage, so I led the class. It must have gone pretty well, because the man in charge then asked, "How about coming back on Wednesday night and giving a talk?"

I thought, "Why say no now?"

I agreed and was expecting a handful of people at most. I showed up on Wednesday night, and the place was standing room only. Somehow, between Sunday morning and Wednesday night, expectations had grown in Simmesport, Louisiana. Me "giving a talk" had turned into a revival service led by an evangelist from California.

When I walked into the chapel, I said to myself, "What have I gotten myself into?"

Before I could start, some ladies on the front row asked me to sing a "special."

I said, "No, I think that's where I am going to draw the line."

They did not look really happy with me and looked even less happy after I finished my message. Let's just say I did not connect with the audience. It was a complete disaster. This experience confirmed in my mind that I was not a pastor.

My reason for going to seminary was to be prepared to do whatever God might call me to do. I had eliminated "pastor" from the list.

I attended Talbot School of Theology at Biola University. Seminary was a good experience. I learned a lot. I made some great friends.

In my last year at Talbot, there was a class called Pastoral Ministry that was all about doing funerals and conducting weddings. I went to the dean of the seminary and said, "I am not going to be a pastor, so I do not need this class. Could I take a different class?"

Having observed me for three years, he thought that would be a good idea. I graduated from seminary in 1980 without knowing what was coming next in my life.

The most important thing that happened to me in Seminary was that I met Sara Netland. Sara was raised in Japan, where her parents had been lifelong missionaries. She was in the nursing program at Biola. It did not take long before we fell in love and I proposed. She said yes even though I did not have any real clear direction in my life.

I did know that I needed a job. I had a friend who was teaching at Capistrano Valley Christian School in San Juan Capistrano, California. They needed a football coach, and so I applied and got the job. Football had been a really important part of my life. I loved the game and I loved coaching. The problem at a small school was that there were so many other things to do.

Within the first year, I became the vice principal for the entire K-12 school. Over time, I handled discipline for a thousand kids, ran the high school, served as athletic director, taught history and Bible, and continued to coach football.

After seven years at the school, there were things going on that left me unsettled. I loved coaching and teaching. I began to wonder about what we were trying to accomplish as a Christian school. It seemed one of the things that motivated people to send their kids to a Christian school was to protect them from a culture that undermines their faith. But sometimes it seemed we were giving kids just enough Christianity to inoculate them from the real thing. I was wondering, "Do I really want to spend the rest of my life doing this?"

One day, I went on a walk and was praying about the future and these words came to my mind: "You are a pastor."

My immediate response was, "Oh, no!"

I may not have wanted to be a pastor, but I realized that was what God had prepared me to be. The more I thought about it, the more I realized I enjoyed leading and teaching and casting vision, and I loved people. At the end of the 1986 school year, I resigned from my position at the school and started looking for pastoral positions. It was scary. We had three kids at the time, and there did not seem to be a lot of opportunities out there.

I did not help myself when I met with Wally Norling. Wally was the Southwest District Superintendent of the Evangelical Free Church of America. Part of his job was to find pastors for churches.

In the conversation, Wally asked me, "If you could do anything, what would it be?"

I answered by saying, "What I would love to do is to be a pastor in Utah."

The moment that I said those words, I wondered where they'd come from. I had never even been to Utah. Wally, who was known to be a straight shooter, said, "You are crazy. Churches in Utah don't grow."

One thing that had piqued my interest in Utah was meeting a conservative Baptist missionary named Dave Rowe, who was visiting my parent's church in Rialto, California. Dave lived and ministered in Salt Lake City. Even though today Dave does not remember the conversation, I was fascinated as I listened to his stories of what it was like in Utah. I had started reading all that I could find on the theology, history, and even the culture of the LDS Church.

I didn't go to Utah immediately. I became the associate pastor at Cypress Evangelical Free Church in North Orange County, California. It was a great church with great people where I learned a lot about ministry from Steve Highfill, the senior pastor there.

There was one issue in my life I needed to deal with. I mentioned earlier that I had a sense of humor that did not fit in with the pastors I knew. I liked to think of myself as "authentic and real." In reality, my sense of humor was cynical and sarcastic. After about a month at Cypress, Steve said something to me that changed me.

He had listened to me enough to pick up on my manner of speech and my attitude, and he said to me, "Do you realize how critical and negative you sound?"

At first, I wanted to defend myself, but soon I realized there was no defense. I was a shepherd. I was called to love the sheep and care for them. You can't do that and be cynical and sarcastic about them. Yes, I have reverted to form on occasion, but that rebuke changed me. God was using this time at Cypress to get me ready for something different.

Chapter 3
Going to Utah

While I was at Cypress, I met a guy named Steve Amy, who had been a pastor. His life and his church fell apart when he went through a divorce. He wandered away from the Lord for a time. It was in that period that he met and married Sonja, a Mormon girl from Utah. After getting married, they realized they had issues and needed help, and they started coming to Cypress Evangelical Free Church together.

Sonja enjoyed our church and wanted to meet with me. I was able to explain some of the main differences between Mormonism and biblical Christianity. At one point, I shared the gospel with her. She told me she wanted to receive Christ and be baptized.

I was shocked. I said, "You do?"

Despite all of my training and years as a Christian, I had never actually led anyone to Jesus. That was a pretty amazing thing. Getting baptized was no small thing for Sonja. She was from a family with deep Mormon roots. She understood that, in coming to Christ, she was leaving that behind. Typically, it takes Mormons years to make that kind of decision. Sonja was ready. Steve and Sonja gave their marriage to the Lord.

Steve and Sonja were also instrumental in getting us to Utah. Steve and I had a standing appointment for breakfast once a week. He had begun to travel to Utah quite a bit because his sister, Jeri, had been diagnosed with cancer. Jeri was also a Mormon, but not a mainstream Mormon. She was part of a fundamentalist offshoot of the LDS Church. She was in a polygamous marriage where she and her sister, Claudia, were married to the same man. Jeri left this group and her marriage.

Steve began to come to Utah to see his sister, and in time, she received Christ. When he came, he would bring her to the Evangelical Free Church in Orem (the church known as CenterPoint today). Before Labor Day of 1988, Steve told me that he was going up to Utah to visit his sister. Without giving it a lot of thought, I said, "If you hear of any churches up there that need a pastor, let me know."

That Sunday, as Steve was sitting in the congregation, the pastor of the church announced his resignation. This pastor had concluded that the church was dying and there was no way forward. The reality was that the church was in no position financially to be able to go out and bring in another pastor. The situation was such that actual consideration was being given to shutting the church down.

As the pastor announced his resignation during the worship service, the people were pretty somber, with one exception. According to the people there, Steve was rocking back and forth in his pew, trying to contain his laughter because, in his mind, he had already put me together with this church. He was giddy. After the service, he told the chairman of the church board and anyone else who would listen not to worry because he knew their next pastor, a guy named Scott McKinney from Southern California.

Later on in the day, Steve tracked me down by phone. He blurted out, "Scott, it's all been settled. You are going to be the next pastor of the Evangelical Free Church in Orem."

The problem was that I had neglected to mention any of this to Sara, the mother of my four children. I got off the phone and she asked what that was all about. I began to explain that there was this church in Utah that needed a pastor.

In time, we learned more about the church, its history, and the financial situation it was in. After getting a clearer picture of the situation, Sara was pretty sure I had lost my mind. The church in Orem was open to having me come up and speak. I wanted to see the situation for myself. So, on the last Sunday of September 1988, Steve and I drove up to Orem to check things out.

My first impression was that this place was beautiful. I was blown away by the fall colors on the mountains. I could not help but notice LDS churches every other block. When we drove through the campus of Brigham Young University, I was stunned. I knew all about BYU, but I was overwhelmed by the size of the school and the obvious wealth the church had at its disposal to build such a place.

As I looked at the students walking around the campus, it hit me that 99 percent of these students were LDS. I began to get an idea of how big, powerful, and wealthy the LDS Church was. It was at that moment that I began to question my sanity. "You are thinking about coming here to pastor a tiny little church that will grow to the point where it makes a difference in this place?" It was intimidating.

Later that night, we met with some of the leaders of the church for dinner. I listened to these people's stories. I asked questions about the state of the church.

There were very few young families in the church. This church had grown old and seemed set in its ways. These folks did not like living in Utah. They did not like Mormons. They had very little hope that anything would ever change. It almost seemed they were trying to talk me out of coming. After that dinner, I laid down in bed and thought, "Well, that was depressing."

I called Sara the next morning, before I was to go and speak at the church. "Do you see any potential there?" she asked.

"Absolutely none," I said. "This is the most negative situation I have ever seen. I will tell you more tonight when I get home."

I finished the phone call by apologizing to Sara for getting her worked up about moving to Utah. At that point on Sunday morning, it was not happening.

As I stood up and gave the message that morning, something happened to me. I looked at the people of that church and had what I would call a "like sheep without a shepherd" moment.

The seed of vision comes when we realize that things are not what they are supposed to be. Vision comes to life when God gives us a picture of how things could be. As I drove home, I had ten hours and 600 miles to think and pray about what could happen in Utah Valley.

I realized that I had something to say to this church. No one wants to go to a church where the people in it hate the people they live around. Churches in California that hate Californians don't fare very well. Churches in Utah that hate Mormons don't fare very well either.

I began to think, "What if there was a church in Utah Valley that actually existed to love and reach out to their neighbors? What if we became a church that existed to reach the people of Utah?"

The closer I got to home, the more desire I had to be the pastor of that kind of church. As I look back at my life and the way that I had felt about being a pastor, I realized that I wasn't called to be a pastor *per se*. I feel I was called to be a pastor in Utah Valley. There is something about the challenge of this place that makes me come alive.

I had not talked to Sara since I had told her there was no way we were going to Utah. By the time I got home, I had come to see things differently. I said to Sara, "I think this might be where God is leading us."

I told Sara about my "sheep without a shepherd" moment. I was excited. I said, "Yes, Utah Valley is overwhelmingly Mormon, but it all comes down to the way we look at it."

I had heard the story of two shoe salesmen who were sent to an island where no one wore shoes. One salesman got there and wrote back to the home office and said, "Send me a ticket home, no one here wears shoes." The other salesman said, "Send me more shoes, no one here wears shoes."

I wanted to be the guy who said, "Send more shoes."

The problem with the analogy was that almost all of the people of Utah Valley were wearing shoes—they were just of a different kind. They seemed pretty happy with the shoes they were wearing. I was not thinking about the obstacles; I was thinking about the opportunity. The great reality check for me was that I knew this was asking a lot of Sara. No matter how passionate I was, if Sara did not feel called to go, then we were not going.

Sara is a strong woman. Sara shows me grace, but she tells me the truth. Sara had never made it her goal to be a pastor's wife, and going to Utah had definitely never been on her radar. I did something that was uncharacteristic of me. I shut up. I prayed and asked the Lord to show Sara if this is what we were supposed to do.

One day as we were on a walk, she grabbed me by the arm and said, "Let's go."

Sara is a beautiful woman. She is also amazingly loyal. I have the kind of wife where people look at her and say, "We are not sure about Scott, but Sara really seems to love the guy, so he must be okay." She has believed in me when I did not believe in myself.

Sara is also a courageous woman. We had friends at the time that asked, "How could you do this to your kids? Who will they be friends with? They will be so isolated." It wasn't just our friends from California that were concerned for us. There were people in Utah that were a part of the church that were concerned for us.

We went up in December to meet with the congregation so they could make a decision on whether or not to call us to come and pastor the church. We met with one of the few young couples in the church, Melanie and Chuck Barber. Chuck and Melanie had been given the assignment of taking us to dinner to calm our fears about raising our kids here. What people did not know was that Melanie was struggling with the idea of raising her two boys here.

As Melanie told us later, she desperately wanted to shout at Sara during our dinner, "Don't come, run!" Chuck knew his wife, and just as she was about to say something, he put his hand on her knee and gave her a little squeeze as a way of stopping her.

Melanie held her peace. The Barbers have remained at the church, and we still laugh about that dinner today. The church called us to come, and we came in March of 1989. We are grateful that we did.

Chapter 4
"You Have No Idea"

As 1988 drew to a close, we made preparations to move to Utah. I was thinking, dreaming, planning, and praying. I am not a guy who is prone to saying things like, "God told me." However, I did have an experience before moving here where I do believe the Lord was saying something to me.

One night, I went out for a walk, and a thought occurred to me out of nowhere: "This is going to be hard."

That began a conversation in my head that went something like this: "Yeah, I know it is going to be hard, but what an opportunity!"

Then these words came to me as clear as a bell: "You have no idea."

I really did not have any idea what I was getting myself into. By making that statement, I am not saying that pastoral ministry in Utah is harder than anyplace else.

I have been asked if I had to do it over again would I have still come to Utah?

Absolutely. I feel my life has been incredibly blessed. I am so grateful I have been able to live in this place and raise my children here.

Many of the things we were afraid of simply did not come to pass. My kids have had their challenges. But all in all, my kids have had a great experience growing up here. They made friends both inside and outside of our church. Today, we can honestly tell people we can't think of a better place to raise kids than this valley.

I also do not believe that ministry is harder in Utah than any other place. I can think of a lot of places far more challenging. What I had no idea of was where the greatest challenges would come from.

I thought the greatest challenge would come from the Latter-day Saint culture we were surrounded by. This has not been the case. The most difficult thing here through the years has had to do with the culture of the church we had come to lead. By culture, I mean the values, practices, and attitudes that were prevalent in our church. That culture had to change. Through the years, it has been a challenge to not allow the culture of our church to drift back into unhealthy attitudes and practices.

I would say that the culture of our church was fairly typical of most non-LDS churches in Utah at the time. Our church had settled into a fortress mentality. Our church was started in 1945 by a group of steelworkers who had come to Utah Valley to work at the newly opened Geneva Steel. They realized there were churches here, but not the kind they were used to at home. These people needed to find a place for their families to worship. Several new local churches were started at that time in Utah Valley.

The people that began this church were outsiders. For the most part, they were unprepared to respond to the spiritual challenge of living in a spiritual environment that was overwhelmingly LDS.

The founders of the church described in great detail the opposition and difficulties they had faced living and raising their children here. As I listened to their stories, I heard about discrimination at work and how children in the neighborhood were not allowed to play with their children. It was hard.

Perhaps the high point in the history of the church was in 1965, when they were able to construct a building across the street from Orem High School. Through the years, I have met lots of graduates of Orem HS and I have heard things like, "I always wondered what that building was."

In many ways, the church was invisible. It was a fortress where people came to protect themselves from the cultural dominance of Mormonism. The problem with a fortress is that people get picked off. Many of the founders of the church watched as their children married and converted to the LDS Church.

The idea of actually reaching Mormons was far-fetched in the minds of this first generation. They were just trying to survive. The size of the church largely depended on whether or not people were being hired from outside the area for work here in the valley. People would move here and quickly realize how difficult it was to live here as a non-Mormon. The question for most of these people was, "How soon can we get out of here?"

This was a negative environment in which to try and lead a church. The nickname that one of its former pastors had given it was "the church where pastors come to die."

By that, he did not mean that pastors actually died here. He meant that pastors became so discouraged after the experience that they not only left the church, they left pastoral ministry. By 1988, this church was defeated, depressed, and, in a word, dying.

Before we even arrived in Utah, I asked one of the few young leaders in the church, Dave Holcomb, to give it to me straight. "Is there any potential in this church for growth?"

Dave said, "The potential is not with the people that are here but with the people that are not yet here."

That struck a chord with me. It was clear that the old church needed to die and there needed to be a resurrection.

We needed to go from a fortress mentality to an outreach mentality. In Matthew 16:18, we have the first mention of the church in the New Testament. Jesus says, "I will build my church, and the gates of Hell will not prevail against it."

In this definitive statement on the church, Jesus sees the church as advancing and moving against the gates seeking to set those inside free. It is Hell that has a fortress mentality. The church is not "endangered," the church is "dangerous" when it seeks to live by the mandate that Jesus gave us to "Go and make disciples of all nations."

Before we agreed to come to Utah, we did not want to take anyone by surprise by the changes that were coming. We wrote a letter to the church. In that letter, I said that we needed to honor the service and sacrifice of the first generation of the church, but we were not coming to keep alive a church that was on life support. We needed to face the reality that this church was dead and in need of a resurrection.

We made it clear in that letter that we were coming to reach out to the people of Utah Valley. To do that, we needed a youth movement. We had to focus on attracting young families and college students. In a sense, we were holding a funeral for the old church and starting a new one. I made it clear that I believed the church would grow, and that we needed to be prepared for growth.

Very few people in the church really believed the church could grow. There were not a lot of options. The people of the church were willing to do what a lot of dying churches will not do: hand the reins over to a new generation. What was clear was that this church needed a shot of courage and faith.

That is why the first sermon I preached was from Numbers 13 and 14. In this passage, the children of Israel had been freed from slavery. They moved across the desert to the edge of the Promised Land. Before they crossed the Jordan and took the land, Moses sent out 12 spies to check things out. They came back and all agreed the land was flowing with milk and honey.

From that point on, these spies divided into two camps. The majority report said, "The land we explored devours those living in it. All the people we saw there are of great size. We saw the Nephilim there . . . We seemed like grasshoppers in our own eyes, and we looked the same to them." (Numbers 13:32-33). That seemed like a pretty apt description of the way we saw ourselves in contrast with the LDS culture.

The children of Israel started complaining and grumbling, and the negativity grew, until people were saying, "If only we had died in Egypt! Or in this wilderness! Why is the Lord bringing us to this land only to let us fall by the sword? Our wives and children will be taken as plunder. Wouldn't it be better for us to go back to Egypt?" (Numbers 14:2-3).

There was another report, a minority report given by Joshua and Caleb, that said, "God can do this. We can take the land." They were right, of course, but the people chose to believe the majority report. God looked at this older generation and said, "This generation is not going to take the land." They ended up wandering in the wilderness for 40 years, and then they died.

They died in the wilderness because there were some things that were a part of their culture that they had brought from Egypt which needed to die. The real giants were not those lurking in the land that God had promised to them. The real giant is the fear that lies within us. Very simply, the grasshopper mentality needed to die. That grasshopper mentality says, "God will never do anything here. If we try to do this, we are going to be devoured."

Attitudes about the place we lived in needed to change.

In Numbers 13 and 14, Israel was blind to the fact that they were about to enter a land flowing with milk and honey. They found themselves pining for Egypt. Yes, they wanted to go back to Egypt where they were slaves and got to make bricks without straw.

I started asking people to open their eyes and look at Utah Valley in a new way. "We live in an incredibly beautiful, safe place with a growing economy." So often, I would hear, "I hate this place. If only I could get back to where it is that I came from."

I started responding by saying things like, "You may want to go home to where you are from, and I get that, but this is not a stepping-stone for me. This is a destination. This is where I want to be."

Maybe the biggest needed change was in our attitude toward our Mormon neighbors. There was this idea that ministry to Mormons was all about attacking them and winning arguments. Christians in Utah had an Old Testament mindset. In the Old Testament, as Israel sought to take the land, the battle was *against* people. In the New Testament, the battle is *for* people.

We came and gave the people of our church permission to love their neighbors. Really, it was more than giving our people permission. We have been called to "love your neighbors as yourself." (Matthew 22:39).

Jesus went even further when he said, "You have heard that it was said, 'Love your neighbor and hate your enemy.' But I tell you, love your enemies and pray for those who persecute you." (Matthew 5:43-44).

Yes, that means loving them enough to speak the truth about who God is and what he has done and the nature of the gospel. It also means loving them and caring about them and wanting the best for them.

I thought all it would take to change our culture as a church was one big sermon. After I preached that first sermon, I was under the impression everyone got it and now everyone was on board.

"Now we can go out and win the Valley for Jesus!"

It ought to tell us something that it took 40 years for the grasshopper culture in Israel to die in the wilderness. Culture change does not take place overnight. We still fight the drift toward negativity and fear when it comes to the place and the people where we have been called to live and serve.

I really had no idea. I thought the hardest part of this job was going to be dealing with the LDS culture that we wanted to reach. No, actually, it has been dealing with the culture of our church and not allowing it to drift back into that fortress mentality.

Chapter 5
Giants in the Land

There was a whole different part of our lives from what was going on at church. It had to do with the reason that we are here. We wanted to reach out to the people of Utah Valley with the good news of Jesus Christ. We were really excited to get to know our neighbors. We wanted to be part of a neighborhood and build relationships with the people that lived there.

Looking back at 1989, we were apprehensive about how people would receive us. After living here for over 30 years, what we can say is that, by and large, it has been a great experience living among the LDS people. They have made good neighbors. Our kids have had great friends. Our kids attended public schools and had good experiences. We have been blessed to raise our family here.

We found a house in a great neighborhood in Provo. Our neighbors were, in a word, nice. We also realized that we had entered into a different world. We had what I started calling "Oz Moments." In *The Wizard of Oz*, when Dorothy wakes up in Oz, she says, "Toto, I've a feeling we're not in Kansas anymore." It didn't take too long for us to realize we were not in California anymore.

On the day we moved in, our next-door neighbor very kindly brought over a loaf of zucchini bread. She welcomed us and as she turned to leave said, "Well, I suppose you are Mormon." That was a pretty safe assumption given that of the 40 homes in the neighborhood, there were no non-Mormon families living there. I am sure that after looking at our four blond-haired children she had no doubt.

When I said, "No, we are not," her reaction surprised me. She seemed not only shocked but delighted. I explained that I was a pastor of a church in Orem. She was delighted to have us as neighbors. Clearly, she was tired of everyone looking and being the same, and she was happy at the thought of having next-door neighbors who were different. Word spread pretty quickly in the neighborhood that there was a new non-member family in the neighborhood, and that I was a pastor.

Then came a different kind of encounter with another neighbor. Like us, this neighbor had recently moved to Utah from Southern California. She and her husband were LDS and had attended BYU.

I asked her how she liked living in Utah.

She said, "Well, I miss the diversity of California and I am concerned that my kids will be sheltered."

I then said, "Well, I guess that is why I moved into the neighborhood, to bring a little diversity."

Very quickly, she said to me, "I am very happy in my own religion." She wanted to appear open minded and tolerant but, in reality, she was defensive.

A few weeks later, I was jogging, and a different neighbor pulled up alongside of me, rolled down his window, and asked, "How are we doing?"

Mind you, he did not ask, "How are *you* doing?"

He wanted to know how *they* were doing in making us feel accepted and welcome. He was dying to know what we thought of our LDS neighbors. He was really concerned with how we saw them.

As I think about these encounters today, they make a lot more sense to me than they did when we arrived in 1989. The hopeful sign was that there were people who seemed to be glad we had come. We were met by friendliness and, in many cases, kindness.

As I think about those early days, I can see that I was way too eager to talk about the differences between LDS beliefs and biblical Christianity. I met a lot of people that enjoyed getting into those kinds of discussions. The reason is that so many of the people here have spent two years of their lives as missionaries having those kinds of discussions with people like me. Being willing to have those discussion is a far different thing than being open to the heart-changing message of the Bible.

There was one other early encounter that spoke volumes to the way that our LDS neighbors saw us. We had another neighbor who had been struggling with her LDS faith and came by to see us. She was really excited to have us in the neighborhood, and in time, we became good friends.

She told us that one of the men in the ward had said, "We will get them." I asked her what that meant, and she told me that people in the ward looked at us and had every confidence that we would convert.

That was a new thought for me. The people in the neighborhood believed the reason we had moved into the neighborhood was to get baptized into the LDS Church.

1989 was a different time in the LDS Church. If I were to describe the way people in the LDS Church looked at their prospects at that time, it would be that they almost had a sense of manifest destiny. They believed they were destined to become the largest, most powerful religious group in America. This was a time when the LDS Church looked at the world and its prospects for growth with unbounded optimism.

In the first year we were here, we went to a neighborhood party and I overheard a neighbor who worked for the Provo/Orem Chamber of Commerce speculate about what the LDS Church would look like in 20 years. In 1989, the LDS Church had around seven million members. He spoke confidently of the church growing to 30 to 40 million members by 2010. There was a sense that the future growth of the church was unstoppable.

Those growth projections have not come to pass, but what has come to pass is that the LDS Church has become powerful and wealthy today beyond anyone's expectations. The 80s was a decade that did a lot for the self-esteem of the LDS people. The LDS Church was growing. The activity rate within the church was at an all-time high. In 1984, the LDS Church's flagship University, BYU, won a national championship in football. The LDS Church was seen as a successful enterprise run by successful people.

As we began our ministry here in Orem, I began to understand that there was a reason for the "grasshopper mentality." There really were giants in the land. They were actually bigger and more powerful than I had originally thought. There were times when I looked at our situation and said to myself, "What was I thinking?"

Chapter 6
"It Will Never Happen Here"

If the Evangelical Free Church in Orem had an unofficial motto in 1989, it would have been, "It will never happen here." At that time, there were churches in other parts of Utah that were growing. I learned a lot from Les Magee, pastor of Washington Heights Church in Ogden.

Les Magee had led a small Baptist church that was a lot like ours into a period of sustained growth in the 80s. Les became something of a mentor to me over the years. Whenever I would talk of Washington Heights and try to give people a sense of optimism based on their example, I would hear, "But that is Ogden. This is Utah Valley."

Within a few months, the chairman of our board at the church, Lee Brown, took me out to lunch. He said, "Look, this approach you are trying to bring here is not working. There is no shame in packing up and heading back to California."

As we talked, it became clear that there was a lot of murmuring and grumbling going on. People were not excited about the new direction things were taking.

Lee had come to me with good intentions. He really was concerned for me and my family. He had seen a lot of pastors come and go. The way it went was that when enough people became dissatisfied with the pastor, they would stop giving, and then the pastor would have to leave because there was no money left to pay a salary. I told him I appreciated him giving me the heads up, but I let him know I was not going anywhere.

What was different in my case was that I was not dependent on the church here in Utah for all of my support. Back when we were leaving California, people wanted to know how we would survive in Utah with a church that could not pay a fulltime salary. A number of people at the Cypress Church made it known that they wanted to support us financially.

We also made connections with JAC and Leanne Redford. JAC and Leanne were former Mormons from Utah who had left Mormonism and were attending Fullerton Evangelical Free Church.

They had begun a ministry to Mormons. This group ended up supporting us through prayer as well as financially. This meant that we came to Utah realizing we were not alone. This group from California had bought into the vision of a church in Utah that existed to reach the people of Utah.

Being supported by all of these people outside the church allowed us to devote fulltime energy to the church. The outside support we received also made people in the church in Orem realize I was accountable to a greater vision.

Within the first year, we started to grow. Then came a defining moment. One of the things I had written in the letter I had sent to the church before coming to Utah was that they needed to prepare mentally for growth. I said, "The building is a blessing, but are we going to build the ministry around the building or the building around the ministry?" I mentioned the sanctuary had pews, and those pews would seat about 80 people. I asked if they would be willing to sell the pews and buy chairs in order to seat more people. In the minds of that first generation of the church, the pews were safe. After all, this is Utah Valley.

When attendance grew to around 100 people and it was clear we needed more room, the time came to sell the pews. As promised, we sold the pews and bought chairs.

The morning the man who bought the pews came by to pick them up, a group of seniors from our church showed up in the parking lot at the same time. They said nothing as I helped load the pews onto the man's trailer.

It was at that moment I realized that things would never be the same. I also understood how hard this had to be for them. "This young pastor from California shows up with all of these crazy ideas, and now he has sold our pews." There was resistance, but that first generation had come to the point where they were too tired to fight.

The important question for us was, "How do we deal with the older generation of the church?" This was something that Sara was a tremendous help in. We chose to love them and to shepherd them. But we had to do that without ever losing sight of the vision.

Early on, most of the growth in our church occurred not from the people of Utah Valley but from the outside. Local computer companies like Novell and WordPerfect had begun to hire people from all over the country, and a number of those families came to our church. In the early 90s, we experienced the kind of growth people had a hard time imagining was possible. As our church grew, we had two building projects to accommodate that growth. By 1996, we were close to 400 people.

At the same time, leading our church was a struggle. There were lots of different agendas. What kinds of practices and attitudes would prevail in our church? There were people that differed when it came to our approach to Mormonism. We were committed to making Sunday morning an environment that was welcoming to Mormons. We did not talk about Mormons or Mormonism. We made Sunday morning about Jesus.

We had some people come to the church who wanted a far more confrontational approach. When people moved in from outside the area, they were often looking for a church like the one they'd left behind. Many of the people that had moved in from other places had strong ideas about church and the way things should be done. They were not going to find that at our church.

Sometimes, it felt like people came to us because there were no better options. It felt like they were settling. Alongside that, there was still resentment from the small group of founders still at the church who would say I had come and "stolen their church."

It was an unwieldly group to shepherd. People had strong ideas about what today seem like minute matters of theology. There were strong ideas about church governance. People would push the implementation of different programs they had seen work at churches they had come from. We had arguments over worship styles. We had conflict over preaching styles. We had personality conflicts. We had conflict over politics. In other words, we struggled with all the same issues that churches in other parts of the country struggled with.

Being an optimist at heart, I believed we could find a way to make it work. I believed that in time, people would buy into our vision. Looking back, there were times where it would have been better, early on, when differences surfaced, to say, "I don't think your vision of what the church ought to be is a 'fit' with ours."

As we look back on that period of time, it always felt like we were running into the wind. Along with all of the issues that come with growth, our church remained very transient. We were a church made up of people where the majority had moved in from the outside. There were a number of people in our church who were here but were also looking for the first opportunity to get out. Sometimes, these were the people with the strongest opinions about how we should run the church.

It was not just that people wanted to leave. Sometimes, the people who wanted to stay could not. In the 90s, the tech companies in Utah Valley that had hired a lot of people from the outside also went through mass layoffs.

At one point, we had 23 families who were working for a large tech company called Novell, and almost all of them lost their jobs when the layoffs came. During that time, we had nine people on our leadership board, and after all of the layoffs, six of them were gone. It felt like the moment we would get some traction, we would face the exodus of some key people.

Over the years, I have realized that you won't survive if you do not get used to all the coming and going. The big question we have to answer about people is, "Do we value them because they help us reach our goals of growing a church, or do we value people because God loves them?" We have to love and shepherd the flock of God.

The hardest departures are those where people leave because they are no longer on board with where the church is headed. When people leave for those reasons, it often feels personal. There is a part of you that feels rejected. I have known lots of pastors and, by and large, we love people. It is only natural that we want people to love us back. There is a constant temptation to become a people-pleaser. You cannot do this very long before you realize you cannot keep everyone happy.

We have to love people but also get used to the idea that people are going to leave. My daughter, Annie, lives in Billings, Montana. She attends a church there called Faith Chapel. Her pastor, Nate Poetzl, said something very insightful to me. "One way or another, everyone is going to leave your church. Some are going to move away and be sad to leave. Some are going to get mad and leave angry. Everyone is going to die. One way or another, everybody is going to leave." That helped. You can get used to people leaving, but it does not change the fact that it hurts when they do.

Chapter 7
Life Happens

After seven years at the church, we faced a challenge that was far more personal. In October of 1996, Sara was diagnosed with breast cancer. She went through surgery, where they harvested her lymph nodes, and 11 of the 13 returned cancerous. It was serious and life-threatening. Our oldest, Ginny, was 16, Annie was 14, Robbie was 11, and our youngest, Christy, was eight. This had come at a tough time in our children's lives.

It was unbelievable to see the grace with which Sara led our children through this time. I will never forget after starting an initial round of chemo, Sara's hair started coming out in clumps. She gathered our children in the kitchen. She then asked her brother, Joel, to get the hair clippers. She didn't trust me because I was a little shaky. As Joel shaved her head, Sara smiled at our kids with a smile that told them she loved them and everything was going to be okay.

In her private moments, there was great fear. One morning, Sara woke up and told me about a dream she had had where it was night-time, and she was outside our house looking inside through the window at me and the kids as we were sitting around the table. We were eating soup out of soup cans. When she woke up from that dream, she said, "I have to live for my kids' sake!" She was not too confident in my ability to raise the kids without her.

Sara lived, and she continues to do well. Today, when she goes to the doctor for regular checkups, she has been told that with the kind of cancer she had, she's not supposed to be here.

That time of cancer drew us together as a family. 1996 and 1997 were rough years. Sara spent close to two months at the University of Utah hospital, where she had a stem cell transplant. I spent a lot of time on the road going up to see her and being at home trying to keep things together with four kids. We had lots of help from people at church.

There was something else that was casting a shadow on our lives. Six months before Sara was diagnosed, my brother Keith, who was a pastor in California, was diagnosed with pancreatic cancer. Keith died in April of 1997 at a time when Sara's long-term survival prospects were questionable.

It was a sad time. As a pastor, it changed me. I had let being a pastor of a growing church in a really difficult area define me. I was getting a lot of pats on the back. I realized through this time that I was a lot of things before I was a pastor: a child of God, a husband, a dad, and a brother. I learned to hold onto things more loosely at church.

Meanwhile, life was flying by. In 1998, my daughter Ginny graduated from high school and went to Trinity International University in Chicago. I realized that we had entered into a new phase of life. Over the next eight years, my children were all going to graduate and, at some point, leave home. I found myself mourning as my kids took wing. I began to think about the reality that my kids would end up living in some place other than Utah. The thought of not being around my kids was painful.

As we entered the 2000s, I realized I was just plain tired. I was tired of the conflict. I was tired of all the conflicting agendas. I was tired of being under-resourced. It always felt like we were just scraping by.

As I listened to pastors in other parts of the country, I would hear about churches roughly our size that had two times the budget. It was easy to envy them. I started to wonder what it would be like to be a pastor someplace else. I began to give into the idea that Utah was just too hard, so maybe it was time to go.

The thing that kept me here was that original vision for the church. I realized what we were doing here mattered and that I wanted to be a part of it. Along with all of our struggles, God was working.

As time moved on, we began to see more and more people coming into our church from Mormon backgrounds. At first, it was single people and college students, and then it was families. Throughout our history, the percentage of "former Mormon" has grown steadily to the point where today, roughly two thirds of the church comes from some sort of LDS background.

As I watched people making that transition, I realized something about them: They didn't show up whole and healthy and ready to be committed members of our church. When people come out of Mormonism, they often feel like they have gone through a divorce or the death of a loved one. They are sick and tired of what they call "organized religion."

We have a saying that "we are not trying to reach the unchurched. We are trying to reach the overly-churched."

Former Mormons feel so burned by the experience with the LDS Church that they have a hard time trusting what they call "organized religion" ever again. Not only that, but they have also been told things their entire lives as Mormons that are hard to shake. One is that you can't trust pastors of Christian churches because they are "preachers for hire. They only do what they do because they are paid for it."

Making the journey from Mormonism to a biblical Christian faith is a difficult journey. We have walked through the journey with all sorts of different people. Each individual journey seems to be different, but all of them have this one thing in common: Everyone making it has a lot to lose. We have watched people lose jobs and marriages and reputations to identify with Christ and our church. It takes courage to walk that road.

That is what brought me out of this phase where I questioned my commitment to our church and this place. I came to realize that when people take that journey of faith out of Mormonism to the Christ of the Bible, it requires courage.

It is a privilege to pastor courageous people. I realized we could not ask people to commit to that journey toward Jesus if we were unwilling to be here for them long-term.

As I walked through this time of struggle, there was a rebirth of the original vision that brought us here to Utah. There might have been times when there have been different opinions within our church about what the church should be doing, but I became clear once again on why I was here leading this church. We are a missionary church. We exist to reach the people living at the center point of Mormon Culture.

Chapter 8
Chapter Two

Despite our struggles, we had seen God do something in a place where people said it could not be done. The church had grown to around 500 people. We had several others on staff beside me. It was at that point that I started encouraging our leadership to ask the question, "Is this it? Or does God have something more for us?" As we talked and prayed, a direction became clear for us. In 2006, we launched a "Chapter Two" vision for our church. The first part of that vision was to recommit to the mission of being a church that exists to reach the people of Utah Valley.

The second and boldest part of the vision was to relocate. We made that decision because we kept hearing the same thing: There is only one spiritual option if you live in this valley, and that is the LDS Church.

It was difficult to find us at our location across the street from Orem High School. The vision was simple: "Let's go from a place where we were hard to find to a place where we are impossible to miss."

In 2006, we found five and a half acres of prime real estate on the freeway, a half-mile south of University Parkway, the busiest intersection in the valley. In this location, we would be impossible to miss.

We raised the money to buy the land. We leased out our old building to a private school and put it up for sale. We began to meet across the street at Orem High School in September of 2006.

We were dreaming big dreams and praying big prayers.

We made another decision at that time to change our name. We wanted to get away from the word "evangelical" because it had become increasingly problematic in Utah. Most Mormons had no idea what an evangelical was. It seemed like those that were aware of it saw evangelicals as a political entity committed to defeating the Mormon candidate for president, Mitt Romney, as he ran for the Republican nomination in 2008.

While we embrace our evangelical heritage, we stay away from politics. One of the hallmarks of evangelicalism is evangelism. We want to reach people from this Latter-day Saint culture. Why have a name that creates an unnecessary stumbling block for our neighbors?

However, we were not just changing a name to change our name. We would never have gone through the process if we had not found one that fit our vision so well. We changed our name to CenterPoint because it reflected our vision of pointing people to Jesus and doing that at the center point of Mormon culture.

Our leadership was all in, but we were surprised by the pushback we received. We had a significant number of people leave our church at that time. Some felt that we should not worry about what our neighbors thought about the name "evangelical." For some, it was more than just the name change. Some were looking for a different style of teaching. There were people tired of the emphasis on building a building. As hard as it was to see lots of people leave, in retrospect this was good for us. Our church began to rally around a renewed sense of purpose and vision.

We had no idea how hard it was going to be to build. We went to an architect and had building plans done for our new location. We rolled out the plans in August of 2008—about the time the economy crashed. Many of those who had committed to give to finance the project were no longer able to do so. We did not have the money to build. We asked the question, "Should we go back to our old building?"

The truth was that we did not want to move back, but even if we did, going back was not possible. Our building was across the street from Orem High School. We had been allowed by the city to add onto our building back in 1995 because we had a reciprocal parking agreement with Orem High where we could use their parking lot on Sunday morning. Around 2008, the Alpine School District made a decision to tear down old Orem High and rebuild it on the parking lot. When they began to build, they put up a fence around their parking lot and all that we had left were our own 90 parking spaces.

We could not move forward to a new home. We could not move back to our old building. We began to wander in the wilderness. Between 2006 and 2016, we ended up meeting in four different schools for worship services. We actually bought a moving van, and every week we unloaded it and loaded it up again. We had to move offices four times.

During this time, we truly appreciated the school district allowing us to meet on Sunday mornings in different schools. They also made it clear that this was a temporary arrangement. We felt like we were under tremendous pressure to find a home.

It was around this time that we discovered something called Sprung Structures. These are basically tentlike structures that are used on a lot of military bases. This seemed to be the quickest, least expensive way to build a church home on our new property. Soon, we found some used Sprung material with which to build. Can you say, "Bad decision?" In time, a significant amount of the material was stolen, and we no longer had all of the pieces to build with.

These were discouraging times. Our staff was incredibly faithful through it all. Every week, they faithfully set up and tore down and packed up for church. The reality was that it felt like we were digging a hole every week and filling it back up again. It did not look like there was any end in sight.

God was using this time to build leaders in our church. One example was our worship pastor, Chris Allen. Chris was largely responsible for moving us in and out every week. Chris is a very talented worship leader, but during that time he also exhibited a gift for organizing and motivating volunteers. Today, Chris is our executive pastor. We did not know it, but God was getting us ready for the future.

As difficult as these times were, we can look back now and see that some of the best ministry in the history of the church took place in those years. During those years, hundreds of people came to Christ and were baptized. We were seeing entire families from LDS backgrounds come to faith. We were ministering to children and youth in an effective way. We saw great ministry happening at BYU and at Utah Valley University. Every summer, we were having large public baptisms in the Provo River, where it was normal to have between 40 and 50 people baptized.

At the same time, the energy expended in moving in and out every week was exhausting. We knew we needed a home.

Chapter 9
Building a Home

In order to find a home, we put all of our options on the table. For a time, we even put our five-and-a-half-acre piece of property on the freeway up for sale. The idea was to buy an already existing building that we could turn into a church. We were not able to sell the property. Looking back on that failed effort, we could only see the grace of God in this.

One day, my good friend Tom Bradley (also the president of our church board at the time) and I went out to our property with fresh eyes. We looked at our land and Tom said, "How can we even think of selling this land? We need to build right here."

Here was this place where every day, hundreds of thousands of cars drove by, a half-mile south of the busiest intersection in the valley.

There was one thing that held us back from building there: We needed to sell our old building across the street from Orem High. At the end of 2013, we entered into an escrow agreement with a funeral home to purchase the property. That sale fell through, and we were deeply disappointed.

Several months later in the Spring of 2014, hope came alive again. The school that was leasing the building from us, Arches Academy, finally decided they wanted to buy our building. This looked like it would work.

In late August of 2014, a few weeks before the deal was to close, we had a meeting with the leadership of the school, and the deal fell apart. I walked out of that meeting saying, "And the hits just keep on coming."

It had been suggested by a number of critics that I had led the church out into the wilderness to die. I thought maybe those folks were right. I said, "I guess that is the way that it is always going to be in Utah Valley. Why would I expect anything different?"

There were other things going on in our lives besides our real estate frustrations. There was high school football. The meeting where the deal to sell our building fell apart was on a Friday. That same night was the opening game for the American Fork Cavemen football team where my two sons-in-law coached football.

Aaron Behm and my daughter Ginny had gone to Trinity College in Chicago. After they got married, they were living in Chicago, where Aaron taught and coached football, and Ginny was a junior high school teacher.

When the head football coaching job opened up at American Fork High (ten miles north of us), Aaron applied and miraculously got the job. He was told he could bring someone with him. He asked Jon Lehman, a former teammate, to come and coach with him. Jon moved out and became Aaron's defensive coordinator.

In due time, Jon and my youngest daughter, Christy, fell in love and got married. By the way, after seven years together with Aaron, Jon left American Fork to become the head coach at Skyridge High School. Jon and Aaron are amazing guys and have had a huge impact on their communities. Today, our loyalties are divided. We have a saying, though: "Two teams, one family." It works.

But back in 2014, American Fork football was still coached by Aaron and Jon. As deeply disappointed as I was that our building had fallen out of escrow, I was excited about the opening night of football season. This was going to be our year!

The game that night was played in the midst of a torrential downpour filled with lightning delays. We didn't just lose to Brighton High; we gave the game away in the last minute. I was miserable. I said to myself, "This is just like our church. You get your hopes up, only to have them dashed."

I saw Jon and Aaron the next day and asked them, "What are you guys going to do differently?"

They looked at me and said, "We are not going to do anything differently. We are doing the right things. We just need to keep doing them and we will be fine."

That was another one of those times when it felt like the Lord was speaking right to me. I went away from that time saying, "Lord, I do not know how you are going to provide a home for our church, but we are doing the right things. We are going to keep doing what you have showed us to do to reach this culture, and we are going to leave the rest to you."

After that loss, the Cavemen did something no one expected them to do. They went through their region undefeated and went all the way to the state championship game.

Something happened for CenterPoint Church during that fall of 2014 as well. That next week, the deal to sell our old building came back together. All of a sudden, it seemed like the wind was at our backs. We were able to move forward.

We got financing from a local credit union and worked with a local contractor. We were able to get approvals through the city. We started building a 27,000-square-foot building in June of 2015. We did a lot of the labor on the interior of the building ourselves. We built it for $83 a square foot.

During these years, it was amazing to see the people the Lord had in place to help us in our journey. Dr. Brent Slife was our board president at the time. Brent not only led our board well, but we also met weekly for lunch, and he became a true friend.

Brent was a psychology professor at BYU. In his last year at BYU in 2017, he was named the Karl Maeser Professor of the Year for the entire university. He also had a private practice as a therapist.

As we met together, there was more than a little therapy going on for me. Brent's presence also gave us credibility with the community as we went through the process of building.

We had our first meeting in the building on the first Sunday of February in 2016. The amazing thing was that the school district had let us know the absolute last day we could meet in one of their buildings was the last Sunday in January. As one preacher put it, "The Lord may not always show up when we want him to, but he is always right on time."

That building has meant a lot for our church. It is a tangible reminder of God's faithfulness to us as a church. It also is a statement to the community. Today, this building is truly impossible to miss. In Utah Valley, church buildings give the church a sense of permanence. It also makes the statement that we are different. Our building doesn't look like a typical church building. It looks more like a warehouse than a church. It is nice, but it is simple.

Obviously, churches do not need buildings to be a church. Families do not need homes in order to be families, but it sure helps not to be homeless. So many people have shown up because they saw the building while driving by on the freeway. So many have stayed because they heard and experienced something when they came into the doors. More than anything, what we have heard people say that come and stay is, "I'm home."

Chapter 10
Junior Varsity Christianity?

What has been the biggest challenge from the LDS culture as we have sought to grow a church in this place? A lot of it has to do with our tendency to make comparisons.

A big part of our story has to do with what it took to finally be able to build a building. It felt like such a huge thing to us, and then you realize that the LDS Church has more buildings in our valley than you can count.

There is BYU, there are ward buildings, stake centers, and high school seminary buildings situated next to every high school in the valley (and the state). At present, we have four temples in Utah Valley and three more under construction. One of those temples being built is in Orem, almost directly across the freeway from our building. The LDS Church pays cash for these buildings.

Unless you live in Utah, it is hard to fathom the wealth and power of the LDS Church. Consider this: *The Salt Lake Tribune*, on January 20, 2020, reported that "since the 1990s, the LDS Church has channeled excess tithing money into a range of investments that are now worth over $100 billion." (Yes, that is billion with a "B.")

The whistleblower who brought the church's financial wealth to light stated in the article that the LDS people could stop tithing to the church today and the church would be able to fund its programs and ministries because of the 7 percent interest earned annually on that 100-billion-dollar principal. As a pastor, I cannot help but wonder what it would be like to not have to worry about the money necessary to fund ministry.

When you look at the LDS Church and all that it has going for it, it seems indestructible. Most of the members of the LDS Church see their church that way. It is simply too big and too wealthy, too well organized not to be true.

As I meet Mormons and talk to them about the church, it is clear that for them, the primary apologetic for the truthfulness of the church is its wealth and success.

The LDS Church is like a state-of-the-art ocean liner. Most of those riding on the Good Ship Mormon wonder, "Why would anyone ever want to get off this ship?"

When faithful Mormons look over the edge, they see churches like ours as rowboats or, at best, small fishing boats. They wonder, "Why would anyone want to get on one of those boats when you can ride up here?"

In comparison to the LDS Church, a church like ours seems pretty insignificant, almost irrelevant. When our LDS neighbors look at us, they care about us, but they also look at us and think, "Why would anyone want to be in a church like that when they could be in a church like ours?"

The best analogy I can think of is that our neighbors look at us as junior varsity Christians. Junior varsity teams simply cannot compete with varsity teams. Junior varsity teams exist in high school sports to prepare athletes for the varsity team.

Mormons see themselves as varsity Christianity. We are the junior varsity.

It is not just the wealth and structure of the LDS Church that allows Latter-day Saints to see themselves in this way. Spiritually, the LDS Church believes that it has more than other churches. That thinking can lead Latter-day Saints to see themselves as spiritually superior.

Years ago, (I cannot remember where I saw this) I read a "Top Ten List" that explains why Latter-day Saints see themselves this way.

10. We are the fastest growing church in the world.

9. We have strong families.

8. We live healthy lifestyles where we do not smoke or drink.

7. We tithe and go on two-year missions at our own expense.

6. Our bishops serve without pay. Your pastors are paid.

5. We have a prophet; you don't.

4. We have more scripture and more revelation.

3. We have a special gift of the Holy Ghost/God's true priesthood power.

2. We are worthy to go into God's sacred Temple; you can't.

1. We'll have our families in Heaven. You will be with strangers.

When someone that is not LDS displays something that is virtuous, often times Latter-day Saints are surprised. One of the clearest examples of this occurred years ago when the kindergarten-aged daughter of a couple in our church came home one day and told her mom and dad that the teacher had asked the class if there were any children that were not Mormon. This little girl was the only one to raise her hand. She was embarrassed.

Her mom and dad went to see the principal, and the teacher was brought in and asked about it. The teacher's response was that she assumed everyone in the class was LDS.

When it came to this little girl, the teacher said, "She is the most Christlike little girl I know, and you seemed like you were the best little family. I just assumed you were Mormon."

She had made the assumption that Mormons have cornered the market on good families and Christlikeness.

Mormons are not unkind to people who belong to churches like ours. On the contrary, sometimes it feels like they are being overly nice. I have actually had them applaud our growth. I heard a BYU religion professor say once that Mormons should be kind to pastors and members of other Christian churches because they are preparing people for the Restored Gospel of the LDS Church.

From an LDS perspective, our church appears to be ministering a lesser kind of Christianity (or Christianity lite). The belief here is that once people come to a church like ours and experience life on the junior varsity, they will jump at the opportunity, when it comes, to join the varsity. The truth is that through the years, many non-Mormons have moved here and have decided to join "the varsity team." In the 90s, we would often hear that the Utah County area mission was one of the most successful missions in the LDS Church in terms of baptisms.

I have met a number of people who have moved here and joined the LDS Church. Some have, in time, become disillusioned with the LDS Church and ended up migrating to CenterPoint. When I have asked them why they joined the LDS Church in the first place, I have heard the same story: if they were going to live here, they needed to find a social network, and the LDS Church seemed like the only one available.

There are many non-Mormons that move here and do not join the LDS Church. What happens for a lot of them is that they, at first, are impressed by the friendliness of their Mormon neighbors. These new immigrants to Utah may not realize it, but they have become the object of missionary affection. They get invited to a lot of things.

When it becomes clear that they are not interested in joining the LDS church, they are often left alone. They find themselves isolated, then frustrated, then pretty soon they're saying, "When can we leave?"

This can be a lonely place if you are not a Mormon. If you live in a community where everyone seems to belong to the same thing, it can be lonely to not have community.

You can't live here and define yourself by what your LDS neighbors think of you. You have to define yourself by what God thinks of you. Our job as a church is to help people define themselves by what they are rather than what they are not.

That is the greatest thing about living in Utah. It is a great place to figure out who you are. You do not have to define yourself in terms of Mormonism. There is an alternative: my identity is in Christ. The call on my life is to live the way Jesus would have me live in this place.

One of the things about ministry in Utah that I appreciated early on is that the Bible makes sense to me here in ways it did not make sense to me before. Jesus and his disciples were not held in high esteem by the prevailing religious culture of the day. When Jesus called his disciples, he chose people that no other rabbi would choose. He chose fishermen and a tax collector. He clearly had assembled a JV team. As the church began, clearly the apostles were not respected.

We are not going to impress people by our religious credentials. In the end, people here do not care whether or not I went to seminary, if I am ordained, or what my title might be. There is only one thing that will make an impression. We find that in Acts 4:13 where the members of the Sanhedrin look at Peter and John and say, "When they saw the courage of Peter and John and realized that they were unschooled, ordinary men, they were astonished and they took note that these men had been with Jesus."

In this passage, the members of the Sanhedrin were trying to figure out what it was about these guys that was so powerful. They could only point to one thing. They took note that they had been with Jesus.

Following Jesus requires humility. I love the statement that says, "Humility is not thinking less of yourself. It is thinking about yourself less." You cannot make it about you. You cannot worry about whether people will respect you. Humility comes from one place. It comes when we see ourselves the way God sees us. When we have that kind of humility, it produces courage.

Sometimes, as we live in this place, the giants look so big. We look so small in comparison. What do you do in those moments? You take courage. You look at verses like Romans 8:28: "If God is for us who can be against us?" We cannot buy into the attitude that we are JV Christians. We have to live with the sense that "one man, one woman, one child with Jesus is always in the majority."

Chapter 11
No Competition

When you look at the property, size, wealth, and resources of the LDS Church and compare them to ours (along with other churches like ours), there is simply no competition. By any external measurement, they win. This is incredibly important to the members of the LDS Church.

As I stated in the last chapter, the reason so many LDS believe that the church is true is because of its wealth, power, and structure. I had a friend say to me not too long ago, "There must be something to Joseph Smith and the Book of Mormon story to have produced the kind of church that we see today."

The LDS Church today is what I would call a giant plausibility structure. To be plausible means that it looks or seems true. The LDS Church looks true. How do we deal with that? A lot of people spend their energy attacking it. I have come to the place where I don't worry about the size and power of the LDS Church. I am most concerned with doing what we are called to do and doing it well.

This is a lesson we can learn in lots of different places, but one of the greatest examples of this is In-N-Out Burger—a popular drive-through hamburger restaurant that originated in Southern California. They are known for great hamburgers and have created fanatically loyal customers from the rich and famous all the way to guys like me. When we moved here from Southern California, there were a number of things I missed, but near the top of the list was In-N-Out.

I would tell anyone willing to listen, "If you want to make some serious money, buy an In-N-Out franchise and put it here in Utah Valley." I did some checking and found out that you cannot actually buy an In-N-Out franchise. Harry and Esther Snyder opened the first In-N-Out in 1948 in Baldwin Park, California. It is a family owned business and remains so to this day. The reason they did not take their company public was that they did not want anyone telling them how to make a hamburger.

Harry and Esther Snyder were committed Christians. To this day, on the bottom of every drink cup, there is a Bible verse. A couple of years ago, I saw a book called *In-N-Out Burger: A Behind-the-Counter Look at the Fast-Food Chain That Breaks All the Rules.* It was fascinating. Their secret to success was simple.

Harry Snyder, the founder, put it this way, "Keep it real simple. Do one thing and do it the best you can." They made great hamburgers and made them fast and never compromised on quality ingredients and great service.

As I read the In-N-Out story, I expected to read about a well-oiled corporate machine. The reality is that their story is kind of messy and chaotic. The founder, Harry Snyder, died unexpectedly in 1976 at the age of 63. Harry had two sons, and when he died, Esther, his wife, picked their youngest son, Rich, who was only 24, to be president. This caused tension with the oldest son, Guy. Guy was not chosen because he was struggling with drug addiction.

Rich did an amazing job. He expanded by adding locations all over Southern California, but in 1993 Rich, along with several other executives in the company, died in a plane crash. After that, Guy took over the leadership and ran it for several years until he died of a drug overdose. Then, amidst all sorts of lawsuits and power struggles, Esther Snyder took over. When she died, their only granddaughter, Lynsi, took over, and she is still president to this day.

Through it all, In-N-Out has not only survived, but it has also thrived. As you read the story of In-N-Out, you wonder how they made it. The answer is simple. No matter which family member was in charge, they never lost sight of their original purpose: "Keep it real simple. Do one thing and do it the best you can."

The family was committed to making great hamburgers, making them fast, and never compromising on quality. Today, if you get a hamburger at In-N-Out in any one of over 300 locations, it will be the same hamburger that was made in Baldwin Park in 1948. It is the same old thing every time.

I realized after reading their story that CenterPoint Church has something to learn from In-N-Out. In-N-Out understood that the competition was not "out there." They were not in competition with anyone else. They were staying true to their vision and values. They were committed to doing the same old thing. They were not trying to beat McDonald's; they were trying to be In-N-Out.

As I read the In-N-Out story, I could not help thinking of this thing that Jesus created two thousand years ago called the church. The history of the church down through the ages is incredibly messy, chaotic. I have often wondered how the Church of Jesus Christ has survived. Closer to home, I have wondered how CenterPoint Church has survived.

It has been messy. If we have done one thing right, it has been to keep it simple and make it about the one thing we were created for. It is about Jesus and the gospel, and reaching the people that we live around. When we make it about Jesus and the gospel, the church has a way, in spite of itself, to keep on moving forward. There is actually something more powerful than all the properties, power, and wealth that could ever be accumulated. It is when the church does what Jesus calls it to do. When the church exists to do what Jesus created it to do, it becomes an unstoppable force.

There is another chapter from the In-N-Out story that is instructive for the church in Utah. Back in the mid-2000s, a fast-food restaurant opened in American Fork, just ten miles north of us, called Chadders. I began to hear people talk about how there was this new hamburger place called Chadders that was just like In-N-Out. Make something great, and people want to imitate it. Nevertheless, I was excited.

I walked into Chadders, and it was easy to see that this was an attempt to replicate In-N-Out under a different name. The look, the feel, even the menu reminded me of In-N-Out, except that it wasn't. My finely tuned taste buds knew the difference.

I walked out and said, "Nice try, Chad."

In-N-Out headquarters was not amused when they heard about this blatant attempt at creating a knockoff. They sued Chadders and won. Chadders was required to change their menu and do all sorts of things to stay away from the look and feel of In-N-Out.

That is not what put Chadders out of business. What put an end to Chadders was that in 2009, In-N-Out decided to come to Utah Valley. They opened restaurants in American Fork and Orem. People stopped going to Chadders and went to In-N-Out instead because that was where they could get the real deal.

Here is the point: To Mormons, a lot of Christian ministries seem to be all about winning the lawsuit. They exist to prove the LDS Church is not what it claims to be.

Such ministries can play important roles. But as a local church, we are not trying to win the lawsuit. Our primary effort is not trying to prove that the LDS Church is not what it claims to be. We are trying to do in this place what Jesus created his church to do. We are making it about the gospel.

Here is what we can learn from the In-N-Out story. When In-N-Out finally came to Utah, they were not worried about Chadders. They were worried about doing the one thing they have always done, and that is to make great hamburgers.

In a very real way, we are not worried about the LDS Church. We are not trying to put the LDS Church out of business. The LDS Church is not going out of business anytime soon. Our goal over the last 30 years has been to do the one thing we were created to do: make it about the gospel and Jesus and seeking to reach the people we live around.

Chapter 12
Less is More

Forgive me for equating hamburgers with the gospel, but I am grateful every time I go to In-N-Out that they stuck to doing one thing and doing it well. Whenever I go to a church and see it is a church that is about one thing—Jesus—I am grateful. Keep it simple. Simple is powerful. The amazing thing is that when we are committed to keeping it simple and making it about Jesus, we make an impact on the surrounding LDS culture.

The reason it is so important to keep it simple here in Utah is because Mormonism is so complicated. When you live in Utah, it's not long before you meet the missionaries. In the typical encounter, the missionaries come to the door and tell you that they are missionaries from the Church of Jesus Christ of Latter-day Saints and that they have a message about the Savior that they would like to share with you.

That message is usually one that is inoffensive, something along the lines that "Jesus is the savior of the world." Their words are usually something anyone from a Christian background would agree with.

My reply has always been the same. "I have received Jesus Christ as my Savior. He lives in me and I am alive in Him. What else do I need?"

The answer is invariably, "We have Jesus Christ too, but we also have more."

Mormonism is aptly named because it is "the gospel of more."

Years ago, I was invited to speak at a BYU world religions class to talk about our church. I described myself as an evangelical Christian and told the class that the purpose of our church was to reach out to the people of Utah Valley with the good news of Jesus Christ.

One young man frowned, raised his hand, and said, "Why would you spend your time trying to reach people with the good news of Jesus Christ that are already Christians?"

I let his question hang there, and a young woman in the back of the class said, "We do the same thing."

She understood that Mormon missionaries do not usually go to people without a background in Christianity. The message that true Christianity has been restored makes no sense to people who have no experience with Christianity.

The young man who had asked the question replied and said, "Yes, but we have more."

At that point, I joined in. "Yes, but we have less. All that we have is Jesus, and He is enough."

Here is the problem with Mormonism: If you say that true Christianity equals Jesus plus more, then you are saying that Jesus is not enough. Colossians 2:9-10 is an incredibly important verse for us. "For in Christ all the fullness of the Deity lives in bodily form, and you have been given fullness in Christ . . ." If you have Jesus, then you have all that God can give you. There is nothing more.

As evangelicals, we are Bible people. We believe that the Bible is authoritative because it is where we find the apostles' teaching. The apostles were concerned that the simplicity of the gospel be guarded. If we hold the Bible to be authoritative and inspired, then the presence of people like the Mormons should not surprise us. In some ways, their message is nothing new. The 1ˢᵗ century church dealt with similar challenges.

In 2 Corinthians 11:4, Paul writes, "For if someone comes to you and preaches a Jesus other than the Jesus we preached, or if you receive a different spirit from the one you received, or a different gospel from the one you accepted, you put up with it easily enough."

There were people in the first century preaching a different gospel with a different Jesus than the gospel taught by the apostles. Much of the New Testament would not have been written if it were not for the fact that there were groups taking what the apostles had to say about Jesus and not only twisting it but adding to it.

There were two great challenges to the early church: the Judaizers and the Gnostics. We see Paul addressing the Judaizers in Galatians. In Galatians 1:8, Paul says, "But even if we or an angel from Heaven should preach a gospel other than the one we preached to you, let him be eternally condemned!"

The Judaizers were saying that it is great to believe in Jesus, but you need to do more: You need to follow the Old Testament Law. You need to be circumcised and eat kosher. In many ways, Mormonism is an Old Testament religion. It has dietary rules and regulations (Word of Wisdom). It has special clothing. They have a priesthood. Mormons see themselves as true Israel.

The other great challenge was the Gnostics. The Gnostics said that they believed in Jesus, but, once again, there is more. There is more knowledge and more revelation. In many ways, Mormonism is Gnostic. Mormonism as a movement began because Joseph Smith claimed to have uncovered more scripture. Mormons claim to have a living prophet and access to ongoing revelation.

The point that Paul makes in Colossians 2 is that we do not need more. Colossians 2:16-17: "Therefore do not let anyone judge you by what you eat or drink, or with regard to a religious festival, a New Moon celebration or a Sabbath day. These are a shadow of the things that were to come; the reality, however, is found in Christ." The gospel is simple. Jesus is enough. Jesus plus nothing equals everything.

It is amazing as you look down through the history of the church how often and in how many ways people have wanted to add to the simplicity of the gospel. There is something about human beings where we believe that more is better. I do not believe this is just a Mormon tendency. Evangelical Christians seem to have an insatiable appetite for more.

Over the last three decades since I have been a pastor, it seems there are these fads that pass through the church where people say Jesus is great but if you want to really do this right then you have to have more. That "more" can take lots of different forms. It can be a certain way of teaching the Bible, a form of church government, a certain school of systematic theology, the kind of music you sing, it can be various charismatic expressions, a certain brand of politics, or how people dress. I could go on and on.

The message is that if you want to be a real Christian, if you want to be an "on-fire Christian," a "mature Christian," or if you really want to "go deep," then here are the things you have to do. When a local church emphasizes whatever it is that gets added to the gospel, soon that church ceases to be about Jesus and becomes about something or someone else.

Being a pastor in Utah has made me sensitive to anyone who comes along and says, "Jesus is great, but if you are going to be a real church you have to . . ."

What is right for a church in the Bible Belt or in Southern California might not be right for a church in Utah Valley. That is one of the things that strikes me about the New Testament. As I read about the early church, I am struck by how much freedom there is when it comes to how we do church.

The form that the church exists in can change. What cannot change is the function, and that is to go and make disciples of all nations. That is the reason there is so much freedom in the New Testament when it comes to form. We are called to go to all nations. The New Testament gives us the freedom to do church in such a way that it makes sense in the culture we are trying to reach.

Let me give you one example. When we began here, we made a big deal about people becoming members of our church. I did not understand the impact this would have on people coming out of Mormonism. They had come out of a church where they had been "members." Having left that, they were looking for a place where they could belong. They would come to CenterPoint and have that experience of "I am home."

At some point, that searching former-Mormon would hear us announce we were having a membership class and that if anyone wanted to be a member, they should come to this class. Then they would come to the membership class.

In the membership class, we would say that to be a member they needed to be converted, committed, connected, and contributing. We called these "The 4 C's." We would hand them a membership covenant and ask them to please sign on the dotted line.

In doing so, they were stating they had indeed been converted and would be committed to our vision, and they would connect with the body and contribute to it. Something like this is standard operating procedure for most churches with which I am familiar.

The response that I would regularly get from people from an LDS background was, "I have been a member of a church my whole life, and that has not been such a great experience."

Many of the people that come to us have, in fact, been excommunicated from the membership of the LDS Church. They have shown up at CenterPoint looking for a place to belong. They are not looking to have their name on a membership roll. They want community. They believe they have found that at CenterPoint.

God is working in their lives, drawing them to Himself. That takes a long time. When we ask them to be members and to sign on the dotted line, many will say, "I am still trying to figure out what I do believe."

Most are not there yet and will say, "If I have to sign on the dotted line in order to belong, then I guess I do not belong."

They walk away. We interrupt the work of the Holy Spirit by saying to people, "Alright, you need to decide now, are you in or out?"

There is a better way. The truth is that people "belong before they believe." That is the way it works in any healthy family. My children belonged way before they believed. My hope in raising them is that they will believe, and that they will be committed to the values and vision of our family. I pray they will stay connected in meaningful relationships within our family.

It does not stop with believing. We also want them to become the people that God created them to be. Part of that becoming is that I pray they will be committed to our family and do the things necessary to make it all work. I pray they will learn to serve and do the things that make our household work.

By the way, we do have membership. It happens when people seek it out. When people come to us and tell us they want to be members, we talk to them about their conversion and their commitment to this church. We add them to our membership rolls. When someone comes to serve on staff or are asked to serve on one of our boards, we ask that they become members. In the end, we are more interested in people acting like members than having their name on a roll.

When we preach and teach, we are all about encouraging conversion, commitment, connection, and contribution. These things oftentimes come slowly in people's lives. When we ask people to do those things, we do so not because we want something *from* them, but because we want something *for* them. Those things are a part of becoming what Jesus wants us to be.

We simply do not believe that signing a membership covenant is a biblical must. It might make sense for churches elsewhere to have membership classes where the goal is to get people to "join the church." We have found that it does not make sense here in this place to do it that way. This is what it looks like to do church in a way that makes sense to the culture you are trying to reach.

The interesting thing is that as we have moved in this direction, people are by and large more committed to our fellowship in serving, giving, and connecting than they ever have been.

PART II:
Understanding Mormon Culture

Chapter 13
Cult or Culture?

One of the most important things any local church can do is to understand the culture in which it is located. Whether you are in the Bible Belt or New York City or Southern California, there is a distinct culture in those places that needs to be understood in order to make the gospel applicable to the people living there. Paul preached the gospel in both Jerusalem and Athens, but there is a great difference between the way Paul preaches the gospel in Jerusalem in Acts 2 and in Athens in Acts 17.

If we are going to effectively communicate the gospel in Utah, we need to understand this unique Utah culture in which we seek to communicate. When I arrived in 1989, most evangelical Christians had a very simple understanding of Mormonism. It was dismissed as a cult. One of the things that cemented that in people's minds was a bestselling Christian book written in 1965 by Walter Martin called *Kingdom of the Cults*. One of the primary entries in that book was a section on the Church of Jesus Christ of Latter-day Saints.

Most American Christians believed that the best way to deal with Mormonism was the way Walter Martin dealt with it in his book: to prove it was a cult according to the Bible. As long as we could keep producing information exposing the false claims of Mormonism, it would be held in check.

Martin's definition of a cult was "a group of people gathered around a specific person or person's misinterpretation of the Bible."

I do believe that Mormonism is built around a specific person's misinterpretation of the Bible. More on that later. The problem is the use of the word *cult*. Cult has a far broader definition than the one Walter Martin gave it. One of the dictionary definitions of the word *cult* is "a system of religious belief or worship." Using that definition, any religious group could be labeled a cult.

There is a more popular definition of the word *cult*. It is often used to refer to a group whose beliefs and practices are outside the mainstream. The problem with the people of CenterPoint using the word *cult* in Utah Valley is that here, in this place, we are the cult. It is the people of CenterPoint Church that are outside the mainstream. It is not just our beliefs that are different, so are our practices. The way we do church seems strange and out of the mainstream to our neighbors.

The term *cult* is not a helpful one in Utah. Here in Utah, Mormonism is a culture. It is a way of life. Yale professor Harold Bloom put it this way: "Like the Jews, they (the Mormons) are a religion that has become a people."

The Mormon people have a distinct way of looking at the world. The local church, in order to be effective in Utah, must be willing to understand Mormon culture.

Mormon culture is a "church culture." They have a distinct way of looking at church that is very different from the way we look at it. People that are raised in the LDS Church have very clear ideas about what church is supposed to be like. An active Mormon shows up on a Sunday at CenterPoint and sees people dressed casually instead of in shirts and ties and dresses. They come in and hear "rock and roll" music in worship and see people engaging in said music by raising their hands. They listen as the pastor preaches for over 30 minutes and people seem engaged. It all seems kind of strange and even "cultish" to them. We must understand that, to them, we are the cult.

We also have to understand that the LDS Church has spent incredible energy and resources in the last generation trying to shed the cult label. Mormons have come a long way in this regard. In many ways, they have become part of the mainstream. I realized that most clearly during the 2012 presidential election. In 1989, the year we moved to Utah, I would never have imagined a Mormon being able to run for president with any success because Mormons still seemed to be such outsiders.

Mitt Romney's star began to rise before the 2002 Salt Lake City Olympics. The games were mired in scandal when Romney was called to come in and save the Olympics. The games went so well that the world was left with a positive impression of Romney, Utah, and the LDS Church. After the Salt Lake City Olympics in 2002, the thought occurred to me that Mitt Romney could one day be president.

Romney ran in 2008 and lost to John McCain for the Republican nomination. Romney ran again in 2012 and got the nomination. Romney lost the general election to Barack Obama, but his candidacy showed just how much people's attitudes about Mormonism have changed.

Somewhere during that election cycle, it hit me that Mormons, without really changing what they believe, have done an incredibly effective job of shedding the cult label and have achieved mainstream status.

How have they done it? Senator Mike Lee, during the Amy Coney Barrett confirmation hearings in 2020, responded to some of the criticism of Judge Barrett based on her active Catholic faith. He reflected on his own LDS faith and talked about how in the mid-19th century, the Mormon people were persecuted and driven out of the U.S. He said Mormons are considered heretics, but they have proven to be "nice heretics." Their beliefs put them on the outside of American culture, but their behavior places them right in the mainstream.

Chapter 14
A Persecuted People

There are two different experiences that we have as outsiders in Utah. One experience we have is that Mormons seem so normal and all-American. For people nostalgic for the way things used to be, Mormon Utah is attractive. I will admit that I find it attractive. There are these moments, as we live here in Utah, where you get the feeling that this is the way America is supposed to be. Mormons are nice people.

There is another experience that occurs when you live in Utah. There are times where you see that this place is different. It is where we have those "Oz moments" when we realize just how different this place is.

The reason there are two different experiences when you encounter Mormon culture is because Mormons are a product of their history. There are two distinct periods of Mormon history. From 1820 to 1890, we have the period of time when Latter-day Saints, by and large, were in conflict with American culture. American culture at that time was heavily influenced, and in many ways dominated, by Protestant evangelicalism.

The Mormon story begins in 1820 with Joseph Smith. Joseph grew up in Palmyra, New York. Palmyra was, at that time, on the American frontier. This was during the Second Great Awakening. During Joseph Smith's youth, traveling evangelists would come and hold camp meetings in the area in which he lived. These were multi-day events where people would go and hear evangelistic messages and get caught up in the fires of revival.

Eventually, those revivals would end and the excitement would die down until the next evangelist came. In time, the area in which Joseph Smith grew up in became known as the "Burnt Over District," because it was said that religion had been burned out of the people.

Joseph Smith's story was that the competing messages of the different evangelists had created confusion for him. At the age of 14, Joseph claims to have gone out to a place that Latter-day Saints call the "Sacred Grove."

Joseph later wrote, "My object in going to inquire of the Lord was to know which of all the sects was right, that I might know which to join. No sooner, therefore, did I get possession of myself, so as to be able to speak, than I asked the Personages who stood above me in the light, which of all the sects was right (for at this time it had never entered into my heart that all were wrong) — and which I should join. I was answered that I must join none of them, for they were all wrong; and the Personage who addressed me said that all their creeds were an abomination in his sight; that those professors were all corrupt."

This is called the "First Vision." Joseph actually gave several accounts of this experience. The account quoted here is the official version, which was not published until almost 20 years after the vision itself. This account of the first vision gives insight into the way Joseph Smith saw himself and the church he was leading at that time.

Joseph and the Latter-day Saints believed that when it came to the churches of Christendom, "All their creeds are an abomination, and their professors are corrupt." With this statement, Joseph draws a line between himself (and the movement he was leading) and the Christianity that was prevalent in his time.

The first vision is foundational to Mormonism because it sets out the founding principle of the LDS faith. Joseph Smith taught that a great apostasy had taken place at the close of the first century with the deaths of the original apostles. The one true church did not exist on Earth until God chose to restore it through Joseph Smith. The first vision is the beginning of what Mormons call "The Restoration."

Several years after the first vision, Joseph claimed he had learned of the existence of golden plates from an angel named Moroni who had visited him. These golden plates told the story of God's dealings with the inhabitants of the ancient Americas. In time, Joseph claimed to uncover those plates. He translated these plates and published the Book of Mormon. This book, translated by an untutored young man such as Joseph Smith, became the founding miracle of Mormonism.

Based on this book, Joseph claimed to be God's prophet sent to restore the one true church. He said that the Book of Mormon was a book of scripture comparable to the Bible, and its existence, more than anything else, proved that he was a prophet. Armed with these new scriptures, Joseph officially restored the one true Church on April 6 of 1830. He was president, prophet, seer, and revelator wrapped into one person.

Shortly after the founding of the church, Joseph restored the Melchizedek and Aaronic priesthoods. Once these priesthoods were restored, the church once again had authority to perform ordinances necessary for salvation.

Many traditional Christians considered Joseph's claims outrageous. His claims made everyone but him and his followers apostate Christians. Many opposed Joseph on the basis of his character and family background. His family had been known for digging for buried treasure, and Joseph had been known to employ occultic means to do so. He had been known as a teller of tall tales, and his story of the way that the Book of Mormon had come about was, to his opponents, evidence of his deception.

The church grew. It grew because Joseph Smith was a man with charisma, with the ability to make people believe. If there is one thing that Joseph understood it was how to take the opposition and persecution that came against him and use it to further his purposes.

Historian Laurence Moore, in his book *Religious Outsiders and the Making of Americans*, makes the following observation about Joseph Smith: "Joseph Smith eventually learned that he had something at stake in making his claims appear as outrageous as he possibly could. He recognized that reproach was one way of being noticed and taken seriously."

Joseph boasted that he was the most persecuted man on Earth. Moore writes, "Sometimes it seems that Joseph's behavior was meant to outrage and invite persecution." When he was persecuted, he would say, in effect, "See! I am being persecuted, prophets are persecuted therefore I am a prophet." This became part of the Mormon DNA.

Make no mistake about it, the persecution was at times real. As they met opposition, the Saints became a wandering people. The Saints moved from Palmyra, New York, to Kirtland, Ohio, to Far West, Missouri. In Missouri, Joseph claimed to discover the place of the original Garden of Eden. He claimed that the return of Jesus Christ would take place in Missouri.

In time, Joseph and the Mormons were perceived to be a political threat. Missouri's Governor issued an extermination order that said, "The Mormons must be treated as enemies; and must be exterminated or driven from the state if necessary, for the public peace—their outrages are beyond all description."

There was a massacre of 17 Mormons at Haun's Mill. Joseph was arrested but was allowed to escape.

Why did the Mormon people stick with Joseph through all these persecutions? Many did defect but, by and large, he was able to convince people that persecution by their enemies only took place because they were indeed the one true church and he was the Lord's prophet.

The Mormon people, motivated by their identity as a persecuted people, became incredibly resilient. Rather than being defeated by persecution, their determination and faith seemed to be energized by it.

From Missouri, the Latter-day Saints went to Nauvoo, Illinois. By 1844, Nauvoo grew to be a city of around 12,000. In Nauvoo, Joseph formed the Nauvoo Legion and subsequently took the rank of general. In 1844, Joseph announced his candidacy for the Presidency of the United States. His ambition seemed to know no bounds.

That ambition also extended to marriage. During his time in Nauvoo, word began to get out that Joseph had entered into marriages with multiple women. Joseph was married to his first wife, Emma, in 1827 but beginning as early as 1831, he began to take other women as his wives. He taught those in his inner circle that these plural marriages were practices ordained by God.

It is difficult to be precise when it comes to how many women Joseph married. LDS historian Todd Compton, in his book *In Sacred Loneliness: The Plural Wives of Joseph Smith* (published on December 15, 1997) puts the number at 33.

This practice was kept a secret until a disaffected follower named William Law printed a newspaper called the *Nauvoo Expositor,* which exposed Joseph's involvement in polygamy. Soon after this, Joseph had the printing press of the *Nauvoo Expositor* destroyed. He was arrested and sent to jail in nearby Carthage. A mob attacked the jail, and Joseph was shot and killed.

This was not the end of Mormonism. It, in fact, created much of the energy and dynamism that exists in the church today.

Chapter 15
From the Margins to the Mainstream

The LDS Church now had a martyr. When Brigham Young was appointed president of the church, it also had a leader with vision and organizational ability. Brigham Young realized that the Saints could not remain in Illinois and survive. In 1846-1847, he led the Saints out of Illinois, across the plains and into what is today Utah. This Mormon Exodus from Illinois to Utah has a similar kind of importance to them as the exodus out of slavery had to the Jews.

With the death of Joseph Smith, the sense among Latter-day Saints that they were a persecuted people only grew. The reality is that in going to Utah, they had left the United States. When Brigham Young entered Salt Lake Valley on July 24th of 1847 and said, "This is the place," he was looking at territory that, at that time, belonged to Mexico.

The reason Utah was the place for Brigham was that it was, by and large, desert. He believed it would be unattractive to settlers from the east. He believed that in this place, the Saints would be left alone so they could practice their faith. That meant they would be free to practice polygamy.

After the Mexican-American War in 1848, Utah became a part of the United States. From that time on until 1890, there was conflict between

American culture and Mormon Utah. Part of that conflict came from Brigham Young's dreams of expansion. He began almost immediately to colonize the West. He sent settlers throughout Utah and also to places like Las Vegas, Nevada, and San Bernardino, California.

The U.S. government realized there was a growing problem. Brigham Young had established a virtual theocracy in the Intermountain West. When the government sent out territorial governors, they would be largely ignored because everyone knew that Brigham Young and the LDS Church ruled Utah.

The primary issue standing between Mormons and the rest of American culture was, of course, polygamy. American culture was dead set against its practice. It was a big enough issue that the platform of the Republican Party in 1856 stated the need to be rid of the "Twin relics of barbarism, slavery and polygamy."

The antagonism grew so great that in 1857, an American army was sent west. Brigham Young, like Joseph Smith, understood the way that persecution could be used to rally his people. The idea of an American army advancing on Utah created an atmosphere of great anxiety and religious fervor. Mormons talked openly of avenging the blood of the prophet.

It was in that atmosphere that the Fancher wagon train happened to be passing through Utah on its way to California. This wagon train, which had originated in Arkansas, was one of the largest and wealthiest wagon trains ever to go to California. They passed through Utah along the route of what is today Interstate 15. Along the way, there was tension between the wagon train and the Mormon settlers.

They ended up in a place called the Mountain Meadows, southwest of Cedar City. There, on September 11, 1857, 120 people were murdered by a group of Mormon militia.

Did Brigham Young order the attacks? There is considerable debate over this question. What cannot be denied is that he was responsible for creating an atmosphere of hostility that led to the massacre.

For a time, the Civil War gave Mormon Utah a respite from the opposition of the federal government. After the war, once again the opposition to polygamy was renewed, and the conflict grew.

After the death of Brigham Young, John Taylor became president of the church and proclaimed that polygamy was practiced because it was part of an everlasting covenant with God.

A number of prominent leaders in the church were sent to jail because the practice of polygamy violated the laws of the land. In time, the property of the LDS Church was confiscated. Finally, in 1890, the LDS Church capitulated. Wilford Woodruff, the 4th president of the LDS church, issued the Manifesto, which ended polygamy. The Manifesto removed the practice that, more than any other, made Mormons outsiders in American culture.

The 1890 Manifesto was the turning point in LDS history. Rather than continuing to be in conflict with American culture, Mormons began to conform to it. They entered into an era of accommodation, where they sought to become American in every way. After the Manifesto, the Mormon Church began its push for acceptance by American culture.

Now we move forward to today, to a time when there has been an LDS candidate running for the highest office in the land. Clearly, the LDS Church has changed. How much? Today, Mormons are embarrassed by a doctrine they once were willing to fight and die for.

In 1998, President Gordon B. Hinckley was interviewed by Larry King. Larry King asked him about polygamy. President Hinckley called the LDS Church's one-time practice of polygamy a "trick of history."

In speaking about current day Mormon fundamentalists who still practice polygamy, Hinckley said, "These people are not Mormons." He had a genuine frustration that modern-day polygamists continue to get press and cast a negative light on the LDS Church. He went on to say that Latter-day Saints are not extreme but "part of the mainstream."

Mormonism has changed. It has gone from the margins to the mainstream. You can see how much it has changed in that before 1890, Mormonism was considered anti-family because of polygamy and anti-American because of the theocracy created by Brigham Young in Utah.

Today, people look at the LDS Church and think of it as pro-family and pro-American. Mormonism changed in 1890 in order to survive. It has shown a willingness to change where it can in order to thrive.

The impact of Mormon history on its people is that they are a blend of both the normal and the peculiar. In one way, they seem so "all-American." In another way, they are peculiar. The normality relates to the recent drive for acceptance, and the peculiarity has to do with early Mormonism's drive to separate from American culture.

The problem for the LDS Church is that they would love to distance themselves from the practices and beliefs that once put them on the margins of American society. At the same time, they cannot distance themselves from those things without distancing themselves from the foundations of their faith. The more that it seeks to join the American mainstream, the more it undermines its own foundations. This is the tension that Mormons live with. They want to change in order to grow, but they can only change so much without undermining their foundations.

Chapter 16
Living with Tension

The LDS Church lives with tension. It has to balance the desire to move into the mainstream without undermining its unique claims to authority, which arise from the early period of its history. This tension is experienced most clearly in three areas.

The first has to do with polygamy. There is no greater embarrassment to the LDS Church than polygamy. Its practice in the church is historically undeniable. Probably the most popular rationale put forth for the practice of polygamy today was that it was necessary because there were so many more women than men during the pioneer period. The realities of frontier life were such that men took more than one wife as a way to offer protection to women.

The truth is the practice of polygamy was not a practical matter designed for the protection of pioneer women. It was very much a part of Mormon theology. In the 19th century, plural marriage was considered an important aspect of a man's ultimate goal of exaltation to godhood.

Polygamy is still very much a part of LDS scriptures. Doctrine and Covenants 132:61: "And again, as pertaining to the law of the priesthood—if any man espouse a virgin, and desire to espouse another, and the first give her consent, and if he espouses the second, and they are virgins, and have vowed to no other man, then is he justified; he cannot commit adultery for they are given unto him; for he cannot commit adultery with that that belongeth unto him and to no one else."

Mormons would love for polygamy to go away, but it won't. Popular culture is fascinated by polygamy. There have been hit shows like *Big Love* and *Sister Wives* that American culture is fascinated by.

These programs entertain our culture, but there is a dark side to polygamy. You look at fundamentalist Mormons like Warren Jeffs, who was convicted and imprisoned in 2011 for his own marriages to underage girls as well as arranging marriages between his adult male followers and underage girls. There are still somewhere around 70,000 people in the Intermountain West involved in polygamy. It is a huge social problem.

Mainstream Latter-day Saints find polygamy and its practice abhorrent. They look at polygamy and say, "This is not who we are." They wish it would go away, but it will not. The reason it will not go away is because they revere Joseph Smith as the prophet the Lord used to restore the one true church in these "latter days."

Joseph Smith also instituted and practiced polygamy. That fact is so well documented that the LDS Church finally decided to openly acknowledge it. In 2014, the LDS Church produced essays admitting that Joseph Smith was a polygamist.

Before these essays, Joseph Smith was portrayed in church materials as a loyal partner to his loving spouse, Emma. Many Mormons, especially those with polygamous ancestors, were well aware that Smith's successor, Brigham Young, practiced polygamy when he led the LDS Church to Utah. Many did not know the full truth about Joseph Smith.

One lifelong Mormon woman named Emily Jensen, a blogger and editor from Farmington, Utah, put it this way after the church produced the essays. "Joseph Smith was presented to me as a practically perfect prophet, and this is true for a lot of people. This is not the church I grew up with, this is not the Joseph Smith I love."

The problem for the Church at this point was made succinctly about 20 years ago when a fundamentalist Mormon named Tom Greene was arrested for crimes related to polygamy. He was prosecuted after he went on *The Phil Donahue Show* and talked openly about his polygamous family. He was a public relations embarrassment for the church.

During his trial, he said something that puts the whole issue of polygamy in perspective: "You honor Joseph Smith and Brigham Young and you hate me, yet I am only doing the things that they have done."

How can you put the present-day antipathy toward polygamists together with the reverence shown for Joseph Smith and Brigham Young who were prolific polygamists?

The next area of tension for the LDS Church, between its foundations and the direction that it wants to grow, has to do with the priesthood ban on Blacks prior to June 1, 1978. Before this time, Black men could not receive the priesthood in the LDS Church.

The priesthood means everything in Mormonism. The priesthood holds the keys to Heaven. All faithful males can begin holding the Aaronic Priesthood beginning at the age of 12. This means a 12-year-old deacon had more status and rank in the church than a faithful adult Black man. The result was that the church had very few Blacks at the time.

Why did the LDS Church change? In the 60s, our nation went through the Civil Rights Movement. As the LDS Church sought to accommodate itself to American culture, many Americans became aware of this ban on the priesthood and objected. There were protests at BYU athletic contests. Schools like Arizona State and Stanford refused to schedule BYU for athletic contests. As missionaries knocked on doors, this view of race became a major stumbling block to getting their message to people.

The pressure to change grew to the point where, on June 1, 1978, Spencer Kimball ended the ban on Blacks holding the priesthood. I had a neighbor who said this was one of the happiest days of his life. He said that people were driving around Provo honking their horns, driving with their lights on.

Finally, this great accusation against the Mormon character, the charge of racism, could be removed. No longer did they have to carry the burden of explaining the church's position on race.

We need to be clear that Mormons are not the only church that has had to account for a history of racism. In 1997, I was asked to speak at a forum related to Martin Luther King Day at Utah Valley University and to speak about evangelicals and race.

I spoke about a trip I had taken recently to Chicago, where I had visited Wheaton College (a leading evangelical university). I was able to hear about Wheaton's roots in the abolition movement and how students and faculty had been involved in the Underground Railroad. It was gratifying to see that it was Christians who had been at the forefront of the abolitionist movement to end slavery. In that sense, I was proud of my evangelical roots.

I also shared that there was another side to my story. My family is from the South. I spoke of my southern roots and traveling back to the South to be with my extended family as a child and hearing my uncles say things about Black people that were shockingly racist. The saddest thing of all was to see how the church in the South was segregated, and how white Christians used the Bible as a way to justify their racism.

How do I explain this racism? I do not in any way rationalize it or try to explain it away. I can only condemn it. Racism is a sin. There is no biblical justification for it. To whatever extent evangelicals participated in or were even silent about racism, we have to repent and say that we were wrong. Beyond that, wherever racism remains an issue we have to own it and repent of it.

After I finished, a BYU professor named Roger Keller stood up and used the opportunity to talk about the end to the ban on Blacks receiving the priesthood in 1978. The question he was tasked with answering was, "Why was there a ban on Blacks in the priesthood in the first place?"

His justification was that, in a way, the Lord was protecting Black people by denying them the priesthood up until 1978.

He explained that the Lord knew there was racism in the church. White people in the church needed to be brought along to the point where the Lord would be assured they would welcome Black people into their midst with kindness. Finally, when people were ready, the revelation giving Blacks the priesthood was given to President Spencer Kimball.

After listening to this explanation, an LDS professor from UVU stood up in the back of the room and said, "Roger, why can't we just admit that we were wrong?"

Roger Keller's response was, "You know why we can't."

The reason he could not condemn those racist doctrines was because those doctrines regarding race had been taught by LDS leaders and church presidents. For example, Brigham Young said, "When Blacks receive the priesthood, that will be the end of the priesthood."

For the most part, Mormons look at the change that took place in 1978 and say that it does not matter what anyone said before then. What matters is what the church teaches now. The problem with that is specifically what was said about race before 1978.

In "Doctrine of Salvation," Volume 1, page 61, Joseph Fielding Smith, the 6th president of the church wrote, "There is a reason why one man is born black and with other disadvantages while another is born white with great advantages. The reason is that we had an estate before we came here and were obedient more or less to the laws that were given there."

Joseph Fielding Smith was talking about a commonly held belief. The prohibitions on Blacks and the priesthood were based on what happened in the pre-existence. Mormons believe in a pre-existence where there was a war between the spirits that followed Jesus and his plan to save and the spirits that followed Lucifer. Those that fought with Lucifer became demons. Those that followed Jesus came to this earth and were given light-skinned bodies. There were also those that were less valiant ("neutral"). These received bodies with dark skin. Because these spirits were less valiant in the pre-existence, they were denied the priesthood on earth. The LDS Church has never denied this view of the pre-existence.

I saw this tension played out in front of my eyes in the early 1990s when I gave a talk on Understanding Mormonism at the Hill Air Force Base Chapel in Ogden. At that time, I brought up the issue of Blacks and the ban on the priesthood and attributed it to the belief that Blacks had been less valiant in the pre-existence.

A young Mormon college professor reacted to this and said that I had misrepresented LDS beliefs. Interestingly, afterwards, an LDS Air Force chaplain colonel took me aside and told me that what I had explained about Blacks and the pre-existence was precisely what Mormons believed.

It was not just the words of individual prophets that provided the foundation for those beliefs. The Mormon scriptures themselves have things to say about race and righteousness. A number of passages in the Book of Mormon speak of dark skin as a curse for sins, as opposed to the "white and delightsome" appearance of the righteous (1 Nephi 13:15, 2 Nephi 5:21, Jacob 3:8-9, 3 Nephi 2:14-15, 2 Nephi 30:6).

Once again, there is a great tension here. As the LDS Church seeks to accommodate and become a part of the mainstream, they find themselves in conflict with the early prophets and the scriptures that the LDS Church reveres.

There is one more way in which this tension between the early beliefs of Mormonism and the desire to be mainstream has played out. This one is theological and has to do with the nature of God.

Joseph Smith expounded on the nature of God in a funeral sermon he gave about three months before he was killed. It is called the King Follet Discourse In it, he stated that "God Himself was once as we are now, and is an exalted man, and sits enthroned in yonder heavens!"

Lorenzo Snow, the fifth president of the church, simplified this view of God by writing the following couplet: "As man is, God once was, and as God is, man may become."

Clearly, this view of God was quite different from the God of historic Christianity, which teaches that God has always been God. In 1997, a book was written called *How Wide the Divide*. It was an exchange of ideas between an LDS Scholar, Dr. Stephen Robinson from BYU, and Dr. Craig Blomberg, an evangelical from Denver Seminary.

In the book, Dr. Robinson confirms the historic Mormon view of God. On page 87, Robinson writes, ". . . it is the official teaching of the LDS Church that God the Father has a physical body (Doctrine and Covenants 130:22). The belief that God the Father was once a human being rests mainly on two technically uncanonized sources (sermons of Joseph Smith and Lorenzo Snow) which have, however, in effect become normative."

He was confirming the historic LDS doctrine of eternal progression.

The same year *How Wide the Divide* was published, Gordon B. Hinckley, the president of the LDS Church, was interviewed by Richard Ostling, the religion editor for *Time* magazine.

This was at a time when the LDS Church was looking forward to hosting the Olympics in 2002 and was receiving a lot of international and national attention. This was an opportunity to erase some stereotypes and put the church in a whole different light.

Richard Ostling, as a part of that interview, asked President Hinckley, "Was God the Father once a man as we are?"

President Hinckley answered, "I do not know that we teach it. I don't know that we emphasize it. I haven't heard it discussed for a long time in public discourse. I don't know the exact circumstances under which that statement was made. I understand the philosophical background behind it, but I don't know a lot about it, and I don't think others know a lot about it."

After the interview became public, there was reaction within the church because it seemed that President Hinckley was backing away from a doctrine the church had always taught. People reacted to such an extent that at the next general conference, President Hinckley felt compelled to say, "You need not worry that I do not understand some matters of doctrine. I think I understand them thoroughly. Your prophet knows what we believe about God."

Why would President Hinckley seemingly distance the LDS church in 1997 from the traditional LDS understanding of the nature of God? That doctrine of eternal progression was something that set Latter-day Saints outside of the Christian mainstream.

President Hinckley, in his effort to go mainstream, downplayed a doctrine that LDS people had been taught their whole lives. This view of God had been taught and held in the LDS Church since the time of Joseph Smith.

The lesson here is that Mormons want to move into the direction of traditional Christianity but can only go so far without undermining their foundations. Mormons want to change but have come to realize that they can only change so much.

Chapter 17
"We're Christians Too!"

Part of that drive to move from the margins to the mainstream is evidenced by the way the LDS Church wants to be identified. When you live in Utah and you meet someone who is LDS and you tell them that you are not LDS, they want to know, "Then what are you?" When you say that you're a Christian, the response more often than not is "We are Christians too."

It has not always been this way. When I had my first encounters with Mormons during the 70s, I would ask if they were Christians, and the response was, "No, we are Mormons or LDS." Today, though, Mormons are adamant in their desire to be called Christians.

In the fall of 2018, the president of the LDS Church, Russell Nelson, made it clear that the church is to be called "The Church of Jesus Christ of Latter-day Saints."

He said that when a shorter name is necessary, it can be called "The Church," or the "Church of Jesus Christ," or the "Restored Church of Jesus Christ." He stated, though, that it was no longer acceptable to be called the "Mormon Church" or the "LDS Church." He even went so far as to say that the use of LDS or Mormon offends God and represents "a major victory for Satan."

We live in a day here in Utah when it is really difficult to know what to call our neighbors who belong to the Church of Jesus Christ of Latter-day

Saints. There have been some mixed signals. In 2011, the LDS Church produced a worldwide ad campaign called "I Am a Mormon," which included the testimonies of famous Mormons. During that campaign, the sense was that the nickname "Mormon" was something the church was proud of.

For the purposes of this book, I have decided to use the term "Mormon" and "LDS," and I mean no offense by it. I really don't believe that most Mormons are all that offended by it.

The Mormons I know have no problem being called "Mormon" because it ties them to their history as a people. At the same time, they also very clearly want to be seen as Christian.

How do we respond to the statement, "We are Christians too"? Here in Utah, the answer to that question is complex.

My Mormon neighbors are deeply offended when they hear anyone say, "Mormons are not Christians." They are offended because it sounds like people are saying that Mormons are not trying to follow Christ and live good lives. That is clearly not the case. Most Mormons I know sincerely want to follow the example of Jesus as they understand it.

Is being a Christian merely a matter of wanting to follow the example of Christ? The problem with that is that there are lots of people (many Buddhists and Hindus, for example) who seek to follow the moral teachings of Jesus, but they do not consider themselves to be Christian.

Being a Christian is not just a matter of behavior, it is a matter of belief. My experience with Mormons is that when they think of what it means to be a Christian, they tend to think more of how they behave.

When it comes to behavior, clearly evangelical Christians have a lot in common with Mormons. Eula Monroe, who was a BYU math professor and a Baptist, used a Venn diagram to explain this idea.

Behavior

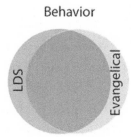

We live our lives in similar ways.

Belief

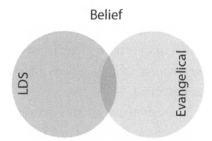

We share a lot of the same words but our beliefs are very different.

There are a lot of areas where we find commonality with Mormons when it comes to behavior. But when it comes to our beliefs, there is a small overlap. Our commonality lies in the fact that we use lots of the same words. But we give those words different meanings. The reason we give those words of faith different definitions is because we have different sources of authority. LDS believe in Latter-day Revelation (which includes the Bible). We believe in the Bible alone.

You see these different definitions in plain view when it comes to the word "Christ." Mormons will say, "We believe in Christ. That makes us Christian." The question is: Which Christ do you believe in? The reality is that Mormons do, in fact, realize that the Christ of the Mormon Church is different from the Christ of traditional Christianity.

The president of the LDS Church from 1995-2008, Gordon B. Hinckley, made the following statement in response to those outside the Church who say Latter-day Saints do not believe in the traditional Christ. He agreed by saying, "The traditional Christ of whom they speak is not the Christ of whom I speak. For the Christ of whom I speak has been revealed in this the Dispensation of the fullness of Times."

What's the difference? We believe that in Jesus, the eternal, infinite God, became one of us. We believe based on passages like John 1:1-3 that Jesus is, always has been, and always will be, God.

When Mormons claim that we believe in the same Jesus, I will ask a clarifying question. "Has Jesus always been God?" As we discussed in the last chapter, the Jesus of Mormonism has not always been God. He became God.

There is more to the question, "Are Mormons Christians?" than our beliefs about the nature of Christ. At the heart of the LDS gospel there is the belief in the apostasy and restoration. Joseph Smith, in his first vision, asked God the Father and God the Son which of the churches he should join. The answer was, "You are to join none of them. For all their creeds are an abomination, and all of their professors are corrupt."

Mormons believe that through the prophet Joseph Smith, God has restored the one true church of Jesus Christ to the Earth, and this church alone has the authority to save and exalt its members. Because of that claim, we cannot be Christians in the same way. In the end, Mormons have every right to say that they are Christians. In order to be consistent, they would need to add that "we are the only true Christians."

My question for my Latter-day Saint friends is, "Based on your belief in the apostasy and restoration, how can you believe that I am a true Christian?"

When I have asked this question of my LDS friends, they will try to soften the idea of a complete apostasy. They will say things like, "You have a lot of truth, but just not the whole truth."

As you look back at the First Vision, that is hard to say. In that vision, God says this about all of the other sects and denominations of Christendom: "All their creeds are an abomination, and all their professors are corrupt."

It was not a matter of Christendom having some truth and needing more. All the other churches are wrong. Not just wrong, but dead wrong. The Book of Mormon says something similar in 1 Nephi 14:10: "There are save two churches only. The one is the church of the lamb of God, and the other is the church of the Devil. Wherefore whosoever does not belong to the church of the lamb of God, belongeth to that great church, which is the mother of all abominations; and she is the whore of all the earth."

I understand that Mormons feel judged when they hear people say, "Mormons are not Christians." What Latter-day Saints have a hard time seeing is how judgmental those statements regarding other churches seem to the rest of Christendom.

One thing I have noticed is how quickly in these discussions a separate issue gets brought up. That question is, "Are you saying that I am going to Hell just because I am a Mormon?"

I think that Mormons, and a lot of other people, have a valid criticism of evangelical Christians here. We seem to communicate a lot of certainty when it comes to who is and who isn't going to Heaven.

Here is what I am certain about. Anyone that is in Heaven is there because of the grace of God shown to us in Jesus through his atoning work on the cross. At the same time, the longer that I have been a pastor, the more I realize how unqualified I am to judge the state of people's souls and their eternal destination.

Augustine put it well when he said of the visible church that there are "sheep on the outside and wolves on the inside." In Matthew 7, we see those that say, "Lord, Lord." Jesus looks at them and says, "I never knew you."

Jesus told the parable of the wheat and the weeds in Matthew 13. In the parable, the disciples noticed that weeds had come in among the wheat. They wanted to try to pull them up and separate them immediately. Jesus says to wait because in their attempt to separate the two now, the disciples might pull up some of the wheat along with the weeds. Jesus says wait until the harvest. Jesus knows those that belong to Him.

Can one have a saving relationship with Jesus Christ and be a Mormon? I believe you can. At the same time, I have to add that this relationship is not because of Mormonism. At the same time, we cannot limit the power of God to save. Mormons do have the King James Bible and know the stories of Jesus. The Holy Spirit has an amazing ability to reach into people's lives and reveal Jesus wherever they are. I have seen this firsthand.

I once went to a funeral for an LDS woman that I had become friends with because we served on a committee together for the city of Provo. It was a typical LDS funeral, until the end. It closed with a man saying that it would only be right to sing "Amazing Grace" to end the funeral. The reason was that before this woman had died, she had read the book *What's so Amazing About Grace?* by Phillip Yancey.

This man said that she was so amazed by grace that she bought all the copies of the book at Sam's Club and handed them out to her friends. He said that at the end of her life, God's grace had made her a new person. To hear "Amazing Grace" at the end of that LDS funeral was not something I had expected, but God has a way of surprising us. We find His grace in some unexpected places.

I went to another funeral for an LDS woman who had fought cancer for years. She loved Christian music and especially liked the music of Michael Card. She listened to it through her struggle. At her funeral, a letter was read that she had written to her husband shortly before her death. In the letter, she talked about her love for her husband but said that her trust and hope was not in the priesthood authority held by her husband but in Jesus Christ.

I am not going to limit the power and grace of God to work through all sorts of different circumstances to draw people to Himself. We cannot judge people's souls. We can make judgments when it comes to issues of truth. The question is not "Are Mormons Christians?" The question is "Is Mormonism true Christianity?" Is it what it claims to be? Is it the one and only true church of Jesus Christ on Earth?

I am not going to spend all of my energy and effort to try to prove to Mormons that they are not Christians. I would rather look at their desire to be seen as Christian as an opportunity.

Mormons are more and more open to listening to music and reading books written from perspectives outside of Mormonism. It has been my experience that Mormons are increasingly open to attending churches like

CenterPoint. Increasingly, I see Mormons with a desire to build relationships with people outside their faith.

At the same time, I realize that as I have conversations about faith with my LDS friends, they are trying to win me. As they do, it seems like our conversations take a predictable course. As we talk, my LDS friends will go to great lengths to try and convince me that we believe the same things.

I have a friend named Daniel Friess who is now a pastor at an evangelical church in Vancouver, Washington. Dan grew up a devout Mormon. He served a mission. Dan and his wife, Danielle, were married in an LDS temple. When they moved to Vancouver, Dan met a pastor and they began to discuss their respective beliefs.

Today, Dan would look back and say that he was in full-on missionary mode. He was going to win this pastor to the LDS Church. That meant that at the outset, he was doing everything he could do to convince this pastor that they believed the same things.

One day, this pastor asked Dan a question that rocked his world. He said, "Dan, how come you are constantly trying to make what you believe sound like what I believe, when I feel absolutely no need to make what I believe sound like what you believe?"

Dan was driving at the time, and the question made him pull over to the side of the road.

He realized that this pastor was right. He thought, "If Mormonism is true Christianity, then wouldn't it make sense that the rest of the Christian world would try to make what they believe sound like Mormonism?"

That was not happening. He realized that he (and other Mormons) were doing everything they could to sound like the very people they believed to be part of the great apostasy. It was at this point that he realized this pastor believed very different things about what it means to believe in Jesus. That was a turning point for Daniel in his journey toward the truth.

To be clear, the desire to sound Christian is not simply a missionary tactic. I have no doubt there is a growing movement of Mormons who long to make it all about what one LDS friend of mine calls "the simple teachings of Christ."

Here is where there is a disconnect. The LDS culture is a missionary culture. Many of the same people who hunger for the simple teachings of Christ are also sending their sons and daughters out on missions all over the world to spread the Gospel of the Restoration. That gospel says that the one true Church of Jesus Christ has been restored through Joseph Smith, and that this church alone has the authority to save and exalt.

The reality is that the gospel the missionaries are taking to the world is saying that "the simple teachings of Christ" are not enough. They have more, and the world needs to hear it.

Chapter 18
"I Hope They Send Me on a Mission"

In many ways, the LDS Church has created a culture that exists to produce missionaries. In 2020, there were approximately 65,000 young people serving missions, and about two thirds of those missionaries were men.

The difference between the numbers for men and women is probably due to the fact that for young women, going on a mission is spoken of as an option. For young men, it is seen as an obligation. Even so, the number of women serving is at an all-time high. There are also a number of senior missionaries usually in positions like mission president.

Before 2012, the mission age for young men was set at 19, and for young women it was 21. In 2012, a significant change was put into effect when the mission age was lowered for young men to the age of 18 and young women to 19. One reason I have heard for the change is that when the age was set at 19, more and more young men were going to college and, after experiencing a year of freedom, were deciding to not go on missions.

Up until the age of 18, a lot of a young man's life is to prepare him to go on a mission. There is a popular children's song in the LDS Church called "I Hope They Call Me on a Mission." When my children were young, I would listen to their friends in casual conversation as they talked about their future and hear them say, "When I go on my mission . . ." It was just something that was expected of them.

There is something unique about our educational system in Utah. There are LDS seminaries that sit adjacent to every high school in the state; where students are released during the school day to take courses grounding them in the LDS faith. I have been able to sit in on seminary classes several times, and it has surprised me how often references were made to missions. The impression I got was that LDS seminaries exist to encourage young men to go on missions and for young women to marry returned missionaries.

Some who have not served missions would say they have had to bear a sense of shame that they have not served. It can even reflect poorly on an entire family. I remember a neighbor walking across the street one day to explain that his oldest son was not going on a mission. Why he thought I would see this as something to be embarrassed about, I don't know.

I asked him if his son was the only one of the young men in his ward not to go. He said he was. I replied that one way to look at it was that his son had the courage to stand alone and not do something just because everyone else did. He told me he had never thought of it that way. I am not sure how much that helped.

A lot of the pressure to go on a mission is social. Most young men feel that if they have not served a mission honorably, it will limit their prospects for marriage. There will be young women that will simply not marry a young man that has not completed a mission. There is also an idea that later on in life, when it comes to finding a job in Utah, serving a mission would be seen as an advantage with some employers.

Missionaries are celebrated in Utah Valley. Every year, Provo has a Freedom Festival parade celebrating the 4th of July. The last time I attended, I noticed there was polite applause from the crowd that lined University Avenue for the floats, bands, and other dignitaries as they passed by in the parade. When the missionaries assigned to serve here in Utah Valley walked by as a group, the crowd around me stood, cheered, and shouted words of encouragement.

Being called to serve a mission is a major life event. When a young person receives a mission call, there is a party held in their honor. The big moment is when the envelope containing the place where the mission is to be served is opened. The people gathered there at those parties believe those missionary assignments are given by divine inspiration.

Before they leave on their mission, there is a missionary farewell at their ward (LDS congregations are called wards). At the farewell, the departing missionary gives a talk about why they are going on a mission and what they hope to accomplish. Through it all, a missionary receives an incredible amount of approval from the people that matter in their lives.

The hard part begins when parents take their children to the Missionary Training Center in Provo, where they will receive whatever necessary preparation (language training, etc.) they need for their missions. The length of those stays will go from two weeks for those in English-speaking missions to sometimes nine weeks for more difficult languages.

The men serve for two years and women for 18 months. In their time as missionaries, they are assigned missionary companions who are with them day and night. It used to be that during their missions, missionaries were only able to call home twice a year, on Mother's Day and at Christmas. There has been a recent change that allows missionaries to call home more frequently.

As hard as it is on missionaries, it is also difficult for parents to see their children go. For Mormon parents, this is all part of a life of sacrifice. Mormon parents look at the fact their sons and daughters serve missions with a certain amount of cultural pride.

In the rest of America, it is common when your typical 18-year-old goes off to college (at their parents' expense) that they get exposed to the kind of hedonism that seems prevalent on most American college campuses. It is comforting for LDS parents to see their kids go off and follow this well-defined path. They believe that if their children follow this path, it will lead them to happiness and fulfillment.

After missionaries return home, they are greeted at the airport by relatives and high school friends. Soon after, there is a missionary homecoming at their local ward. Those years have a huge impact on the missionary.

After the missionary serves a mission and comes home, they do so as a changed person. Those friendships are not the same. Having served their mission honorably, the returned missionary now is expected to pursue goals like getting an education, finding a worthy mate they can marry in the temple, starting a family, and setting out on a career path.

I have heard returned missionaries say that their missions were the best two years of their lives. The reason for that, for a lot of returned missionaries, is that they gained experience and a skill set that helped them later on in life. Along with that, there is a sense they are doing something that makes an eternal difference.

Helping people to gain a testimony that the LDS Church is the one true church is what LDS missions are all about. A testimony has to do with how someone comes to know that the LDS Church is the one true church. Some returned missionaries will say the most important thing that happened on their mission was not so much the people that they converted; it was that *they* were converted on their mission.

As you watch this whole missionary culture function, you realize how much of the responsibility for the advancement of the LDS Church depends on missionaries. There was an article written in *The Atlantic Monthly* in 2014 that put it succinctly: "Putting Eternal Salvation in the Hands of 19-Year-Old Missionaries." The article states the reality that the growth of the church depends on the activity and effectiveness of these young men and women.

A young man named Brendan, who became a part of our church back in the 90s, related a story to me from his mission in Texas. He excelled as a missionary to the point where he was made a zone leader responsible for other missionaries. At the beginning of his mission, he was asked by the mission president what his goals were for his mission. He said that he was "looking forward to teaching people about the Savior." His mission president said, "Elder, you are not here to teach but to baptize."

LDS missionaries go door-to-door seeking out people willing to take "the missionary discussions." The idea behind these discussions is not to have a free-ranging discussion on matters related to the gospel. They are designed to lead the investigator into baptism.

There is pressure put on missionaries for results. These high expectations create stress. That stress is creating cracks in the missionary culture. More and more missionaries who have gone out on missions are coming home early.

Jana Reiss, in her new book *The Next Mormons*, reports that fully one third of millennial Mormons who go out and serve missions end up coming home early. The number one reason missionaries come home early is because of mental health issues, usually anxiety.

When a missionary comes home early, many do so with a sense of failure. People sometimes assume the worst. Early return missionaries have a difficult time assimilating back into their local wards. Some would say that the sense of shame from coming home early is worse than if they had never gone at all. The LDS Church is doing things to help with the stress, like allowing more contact for missionaries with their families. There is also talk of shortening missions.

My sense is that attitudes about missions are changing. The current group of young people graduating from high school seems far more ambivalent about serving a mission than they used to.

I have sensed that change as I have had opportunities over the years to go into high school classes at the local public high schools as a guest speaker. I usually begin my talk by trying to help them understand that Utah Valley is a very unique place. I try to point out that uniqueness by asking the question, "What are your plans after you graduate from high school?"

Years ago, almost all the young men would eagerly raise their hands and tell me that they were going to serve a church mission. After class, I would even have students bring me their copies of the Book of Mormon and ask if I had ever read it.

In 2018, I spoke to a class at a high school in Orem and asked what they were going to do after graduation. I was surprised when I heard responses that would be similar to what graduating seniors anywhere would say. There were things like: Go to college, get a job, etc.

I kept probing to see if anyone would mention going on a mission. Finally, I just asked the question, "Okay, is anyone here planning on going on a mission?"

Seven out of the 30 students in the class raised their hands. In that moment, I realized something had changed. I wondered if this class might have been an outlier. In the fall of 2019, I asked the same question at a similar class at a different school and had a very similar response.

The reality could be that the number of young people who ended up serving missions might be quite a bit higher than the number who actually raised their hands on those two occasions. What I could not fail to see is there has been a change when it comes to the level of enthusiasm young people have when it comes to serving a mission.

Chapter 19
"Families are Forever"

There is a message that the LDS Church has charged its missionaries to take to the world: "Heavenly Father has provided through the LDS Church a way for families to be together forever." There is a poster I have seen in LDS bookstores that says a missionary is "someone willing to spend two years of their life so that you can be together with your family forever."

Mormonism takes one of the best things in this life, family, and says you can have that for all eternity. In a world where the family unit is crumbling, this is an attractive message. It takes the greatest pain in life, separation from those we love, and it gives hope that we will be with those family members in Heaven.

Stephen Robinson, in *How Wide the Divide?*, explains how the LDS view of God is tied up in this. "LDS believe in the literal fatherhood of God and the brotherhood of humanity. We believe that God and humans are the same species of being and that all men and women were His spiritual offspring in a pre-mortal existence. The main purpose of the gospel of Christ is not so much to get us to heaven as it is to get us home."

When Robinson says that God and human beings are the same species of being, it means the difference between God and human beings is a matter of degree in terms of progression. In traditional Christian theology, God is completely "other." God does not exist the way that anything else in the Universe exists. God is not a space, time, or matter being. God created space, time, and matter.

LDS theology, in effect, deifies the family. Robinson goes on to say, "We also believe that human families that come to Christ jointly can, through living and obeying Christ's gospel, be sealed together forever, hence the LDS slogan 'Families are forever.' Finally, LDS believe that God intends through the fullness of the gospel to make us what Christ is and to share with the most faithful of His children the blessings, powers, and glories of eternity." (Stephen Robinson, *How Wide the Divide?*, pages 18 and 19.

For Mormons, God is literally our heavenly father, and there is a heavenly mother. Our spirits were born in a pre-existence to these heavenly parents. Coming to this Earth is a test to see if we can live worthily in such a way that we can return to our heavenly father. Theology affects culture. Because of this, Mormons emphasize strong families.

It has also meant traditionally that LDS families are larger than families of other faiths. In my early years in Utah, it was explained to me that it was the duty of married couples to have as many children as they could because there are "spirit children" that need bodies and families in order to begin their progression.

These ideas are powerful in the mind of a Mormon. To be able to be married and have their family together with them for all eternity is compelling to Latter-day Saints. Along with that, the idea that one could progress to the point where one is able to do something someplace else in the Universe like what God has done here is equally compelling.

But there are problems when it comes to the concept of having your family together forever. I think about a picture I have with my son on one side of me and my father on the other side. Imagine that we were all faithful Mormons married in the temple, each with our own families. Who will I be in Heaven? Will I be my father's son or my son's father? How can my dad be together with his family and me be together with my family? Now that my son has his own family, how can he be together with me?

Families work the way that they work here on Earth because one generation follows after the other. In Heaven, all of the generations exist side by side.

As you look at the Bible, Jesus said nothing about families being together forever. In fact, he said the opposite. "At the resurrection people will neither marry nor be given in marriage." (Matthew 22:30).

There is family in Heaven, but there is one family. It is the family of God. Marriage on Earth is a picture of a greater reality, and that is the relationship between the church and Christ. Those that belong to Jesus by faith are called the Bride of Christ.

The idea that Latter-day Saints can be with their families forever holds LDS culture together. "To enjoy this blessing, we must be married in the temple. When people are married outside the temple, the marriage ends when one of the partners dies . . . If we keep our covenants with the Lord, our families will be united eternally as husband, wife, and children. Death cannot separate us." (Gospel Principles, 2009 ed., p. 209).

You can see the importance of this idea in the way that the church spends its resources. LDS temples are a prominent feature of the landscape wherever they are found. They are imposing. They are buildings that make a statement.

Temple building is important to the church, and that is especially true here in Utah. Whenever a community gets one, real estate values around it go up. People want to live near them.

There are now over 200 temples either operating, announced, or under construction around the world. These temples are placed all over the world so that Mormons, wherever they live, can have access to these places where ordinances can be performed that keep families together forever. Normal marriages end in death. Marriage in the temple lasts for eternity.

This gives the church tremendous power in the lives of its members. If you want to be with your family forever, you have to go to the temple. In order to go into the temple, you have to have a "temple recommend." In order to get a temple recommend, you need to, among other things, be faithful in tithing, obey the word of wisdom, (no coffee, tea, tobacco, or alcohol), obey the law of chastity, and be faithful in church attendance. To get a temple recommend, there are up to 15 questions that the interviewer (bishop) can ask related to these and other areas of church involvement.

Without a temple recommend, you cannot enter the temple. What that means is that non-Mormon parents, former Mormons, or Mormons that are not worthy enough to have a temple recommend, are not allowed to be a part of their own children's weddings. The bottom line is that there is tremendous pressure to remain temple-worthy so that you can be a part of those things.

What happens when someone leaves the church or is no longer temple-worthy and has no desire to live the kind of life that would make them temple-worthy? Families are separated. I know a lot of LDS families. It seems like in all of those families, there is at least one child, often more, who no longer consider themselves to be Mormon.

In practical terms, what that means for parents is that they will not be together forever with their whole families. There will always be an empty seat in Heaven where that member of the family was supposed to be. Here is what that means for many parents: Rather than my family being together forever, we will be separated.

Chapter 20
Leaving Mormonism

The LDS Church is hard to leave. I found a quote from an LDS sociologist years ago that goes like this: "The child of a Mormon family undergoes what must be the most powerful indoctrination of any society. So much so that in adult life that child is incapable of admitting publicly and sometimes not even to themselves that they do not believe in some of or even in all of the basic teachings of the church."

Family pressure and the fear of social ostracism is so great that it has not been uncommon for people to remain active in their church even though they no longer believe in the truth of what the LDS Church teaches.

Thomas Stewart Ferguson was a classic example of this. Ferguson was the founder of FARMS (the Foundation of Ancient Research and Mormon Studies). He founded FARMS because early in his professional life he made it his goal to prove the Book of Mormon to be true. He began to take trips down to Central America because he believed that was where the Book of Mormon lands were.

However, after multiple excursions to Central America, he became convinced there was no archaeological evidence there for the Book of Mormon. In time, he came to a point where he no longer believed in the truth claims of Mormonism, and yet he remained in the LDS Church.

Someone asked him, "Why do you remain a Mormon?"

His reply was "It's the best fraternity that I know of."

Ferguson's story is not uncommon.

Not too long after we moved into our new church building in 2016, I had a man drop by and ask for a tour of our building. It was clear very quickly as we walked around the building that he wanted more than a tour. He wanted to talk.

He explained that he no longer believed in the LDS Church. He was intrigued by what we were doing at CenterPoint and seemed interested in visiting. His problem was that he was active in the LDS Church with a family deeply invested in the church. His wife was a true-blue Mormon. They had a son serving a mission.

He wanted to live authentically. He wanted to explore what it would look like to have a relationship with Christ outside of Mormonism. He was lonely and looking for fellowship. The problem was how would he have this conversation with his wife?

We met together again and explored different ways he could talk to his wife and family about what he really believed. His wife later found out that he had met with me and that I was a pastor. She made it clear that she looked at it as if he were cheating on her.

The efforts he made to have an honest conversation with her about where he was in his faith ended in futility. It was clear that for him to leave the church would mean losing his family. I love this guy, and my heart breaks for him. As far as I know, he continues to be active in the LDS Church. His story is not uncommon.

There are a hundred hooks that keep people in the church. Someone leaving the LDS Church denies their heritage. They get blamed for breaking up the family unit. People's employment and financial lives are often dependent on their standing in the church. Standing and social status within the community are tied to activity in the church.

The LDS Church itself also makes it difficult to leave. BYU is a huge reality in our valley. At BYU there are some non-Mormon students, but over 99 percent of the students are Latter-day Saints. If a student enters

BYU as a Mormon but then makes it clear he or she is leaving the church by changing their religious affiliation, the policy has been that they will no longer be able to continue at BYU. We have had numerous BYU students who have begun to attend our church and have had to confront this reality. Similarly, if a BYU employee leaves the church, they will lose their job.

It is hard to describe to people who live outside of this valley the amount of pressure that is on active Latter-day Saints to remain in the LDS Church. Despite this pressure, there is something that is going on that cannot be denied. More and more people are leaving the LDS Church.

In late 2011, Marlin K. Jensen, a general authority and church historian, said that not since the Saints left Kirtland, Ohio, has the church experienced such a period of apostasy. In the 1970s and 1980s, there were incredibly high retention rates in the LDS Church. In that era, only about 10 percent of members raised LDS no longer viewed themselves as LDS. Today, that number has risen, in one survey, to 36 percent.

Having said that, please understand that the LDS Church in many ways is as dominant as ever. The people in my neighborhood are overwhelmingly active in the church. Still, there is no doubt that people are leaving in greater and greater numbers. The greatest evidence of that for us is the steady stream of people we have seen in the last five years showing up at CenterPoint wondering if there is life after Mormonism.

There also seems to be a loosening of some of the controls that have traditionally kept people in the church. What happens at BYU is indicative of a lot of what is happening throughout the church. The policy, which says that students who disaffiliate from the LDS Church lose their status as students at BYU, is unchanged. However, the application of that policy seems to have softened. Students who have left the LDS Church and want to remain at BYU have usually found a way to do so. A lot of what happens to students who leave the church will depend on the bishops in their student wards.

Throughout the church, members talk about playing "bishop roulette." Will you get a bishop that goes by the book, or will you get a bishop that has a more open, understanding approach?

I actually had the bishop of a BYU student ward call me a few years ago about two African American LDS students who were attending our church. These students were supposed to be in his ward.

He called me and asked if they were attending church at CenterPoint. When I hesitated to answer, he said, "Don't worry, I am not trying to get them in trouble, I just want to know that they are going to church somewhere."

I told him that they were coming to CenterPoint, and he signed their ecclesiastical endorsements and they remained students and ultimately graduated from BYU.

There are other signs that attitudes are changing among Mormons about family members who leave the church. In our early years, it was clear that faithful LDS parents could not think of anything worse than for a family member to leave the church and come to a church like ours.

Our dear friend, LeAnn Redford, tells the story of going to her father and telling him that she had found faith in Christ, and that she was attending an evangelical church. Her father had already experienced pain as a parent from some bad choices made by his children. When he received this news from LeAnn, he said, "You have hurt me more than all the rest. It would have been better for a millstone to be tied around your neck and you be dropped in the deepest part of the sea."

That was over 30 years ago. Contrast that with a conversation I had not too long ago with a BYU professor. He has a grown daughter who no longer considers herself to be Mormon. This daughter is married with children, and they do not attend church anywhere.

This professor told me of a conversation with his wife where she said, "I am sad that our children are being raised without Jesus." She said that she wished they would find a good evangelical church to go to so at least their grandkids would know about Jesus. That was unheard of years ago, but now these kinds of conversations are not uncommon.

Make no mistake about it, we still see lots of extreme reactions from family members when people leave the LDS Church and begin attending CenterPoint. Making this decision is still costly. People are still risking family relationships, jobs, and social standing to make this decision. At the same time, the number of people leaving the LDS Church and showing up at churches like ours is growing throughout the state of Utah.

It is still extremely difficult to leave. People go through stages where they feel a deep sense of loss. They experience grief, anger, and fear. We realize that it takes time. The more people leave, the easier it is for others to leave.

The people we are ministering to have lived their entire lives being pressured by their religion. One of the things we tell people who show up is that our name is not Center-Pressure. It is CenterPoint.

"We are not going to push you or pressure you. We are going to point you to Jesus."

The good news in Utah is that many former Mormons have found faith in Christ. However, most former Mormons have taken a different route.

Hannah Miet wrote a cover story for *Newsweek* magazine for the January 30, 2014, edition entitled, "When the Saints Go Marching Out." By then, the exodus out of the LDS Church had reached a point where national media had noticed. One of the things the article focused on is how "post Mormons" are finding community, having left the community they once experienced in the LDS Church. The question is: Where are they finding it?

The article describes a gathering of post Mormons where the activity of the meeting was centered on teaching people how to drink alcohol. "While the leader extols the virtues of rum, volunteers pass around antique silver trays filled with thimble-sized rum-and-cokes and piña coladas. The samples are served in official LDS sacrament cups. The leader, wearing a black T-shirt . . . with the phrase 'PostMo and proud' demonstrates how to properly take a shot. In one swift motion, she pulls back her hair, tilts her head back, swallows and then slams the empty glass down. In unison, the group follows her lead."

Here is what was interesting about this article. There was not one mention of people leaving Mormonism and becoming a part of any other faith community.

To be sure, this is something that is not just true for the LDS Church. Throughout American culture, the fastest growing category when it comes to religious affiliation are the "Nones." These are people that reject any religious affiliation.

It is understandable that when people leave the LDS Church they do not run to some other church. When people leave Mormonism, they tend to believe that "Either nothing is true, or everything is true." Mormons go through their lives communicating with certainty that "I know this church is true." After realizing it isn't true, they find it easier to say, "I don't believe in anything!" or "There's truth in everything!"

They have spent so much time defending the idea that the LDS Church is the one true church, they find it difficult to ever trust anyone or anything again.

You can leave Mormonism, but some of the ideas never leave you. There are ideas taught in Mormonism that are in conflict with historic Christianity: "I cannot trust the Bible," "I cannot understand the Trinity, therefore I cannot believe in it," "I cannot accept salvation by faith alone."

I heard a quote years ago and have never been able to find the source. It came from a 19th century LDS missionary. "Give me someone for an evening and I will either make a Mormon out of them or make it so that they are no good for any other religion."

Mormons like to say that "when people leave the church, they cannot leave it alone." People who leave the LDS Church sometimes spend the rest of their lives attacking it and fighting it. As a church, we do not want people to spend the rest of their lives looking in the rearview mirror. We want them to turn to Jesus and follow Him.

Here is the great opportunity we have with people that have come out of Mormonism. For many of them, it is like there have been two towers in their life. There is the Mormon tower that includes the Book of Mormon, Joseph Smith, and all of the things related to the truth claims of Mormonism. That can be a really big tower.

When that tower crumbles, there is another tower. Call it the "Jesus Tower." Mormons have been exposed to Jesus. Yes, we know that it is a different Jesus. But Mormons have been exposed to the Jesus of the New Testament.

They know the stories. They believe in the miracles. They believe in the Resurrection. There is something about Jesus that they can't let go of. People are hungry for a life that only Jesus can bring. They are not finding that life in the LDS Church. There is this longing on the part of lots of people that have been raised LDS to know Jesus. The question is, "How do we help them?"

PART III:
What Would
Jesus Do?

Chapter 21
The Challenges are Real

Every year, there are all sorts of pastors conferences presenting models to pastors of different ways to "do church." Among others, I have been to conferences at places like Willow Creek and Saddleback. There are all sorts of best practices that we have learned from these and other churches throughout the country. At the same time, things that work elsewhere do not always work here. This place is different.

Recently, I heard about one of the largest churches in America sending a team to plant a church in a Mormon-dominated community. They had more than sufficient financial resources. They brought in gifted leaders to direct the effort. They launched the church, and within a year they shut it down.

A friend of mine who is a pastor in Utah spent some time with the individual who gave oversight to this church-planting effort. When he was asked what happened to this church plant, the reply was, "The first thing we realized is that this Mormon thing is real."

Yes, it is real. As we prepared to come to Utah over 30 years ago, we began to pray and to ask a question: "What would Jesus do?"

In Acts 20:28, the Apostle Paul reminds the leaders of the church in Ephesus to "be shepherds of the church of God which He bought with His blood." This passage is clear on two things. The church really does belong to Jesus, and He wants it to be shepherded. How would Jesus shepherd a church located at the center point of a religious culture like that of Utah Valley?

Historically, local churches like ours in Utah have had different responses to being placed in this context. One response was the fortress mentality that was prevalent in our church when we arrived.

Another approach is to make a local church all about winning the argument. There have been churches that make it all about proving that the LDS Church is not true.

In these churches, the differences between biblical Christianity and Mormonism are discussed openly from the pulpit on Sunday mornings. When faithful Mormons visit churches where these doctrinal comparisons are made, they feel persecuted. They are able to say, "The true church has always been persecuted. We are being persecuted, therefore we must be the one true church."

Even when people have left the LDS Church and no longer believe it, they struggle when they attend churches that talk about the LDS Church. It is sort of like what happens when other people talk about my family. It is okay for me to talk about them, but I don't want to hear you talk about them.

In our early years, these kinds of churches tended to be more prevalent in Utah. Today, there is a different tendency. It is easy to just try and get along and blur the lines between the LDS Church and biblical Christianity. This plays into the spirit of the age. We live in a spiritual environment in America where it becomes increasingly difficult to talk about religious differences.

There is a hyper-sensitivity to any discussion of religion because everyone knows that religion divides people. The truth is that around the world, people will kill one another over religion. Our culture has a solution to that problem. It is to say all religions are equally true and equally false. Our culture believes that the great problem with religion is when people believe theirs is the only true religion.

An example of how far our culture has gone in this regard occurred back in January of 2015 when gunmen entered the Paris offices of a satirical French magazine called *Charlie Hebdo*. Prior to this, *Charlie Hebdo* had featured a cartoon mocking the Prophet Muhammad.

Upon entering the office, one of the gunmen said to a female writer for the newspaper, "I'm not going to kill you because you're a woman and we do not kill women, but you must convert to Islam. Read the Qur'an and cover yourself." He then shouted "Allahu Akbar" and continued on his rampage.

This woman, Sigolène Vinson, survived. Her account was posted on the *New York Times* website. Within three hours, her account was changed by the *Times* to: "Don't be afraid. Calm down. I won't kill you. You're a woman. Think about what you're doing. It's not right."

The difference in the two quotes is that in the edited quote, all reference to Islam is removed.

Why was the quote changed? My sense would be that the *New York Times* did not want its readers to get the idea that the problem is any one religion. The problem is with all religion, especially when people take their religion too seriously and think that theirs is the only true faith.

Tolerance is not a matter of believing that everything is equally true and equally false. Tolerance is where I respect and even defend your right to believe what you want to believe, even though I believe that you are sincerely wrong.

The problem with American Christianity is not that we take our faith too seriously. It is that we don't take our faith seriously enough. We have to take Jesus seriously when he says, "Love your neighbor as yourself . . . Love your enemies . . . Do good to those who persecute you . . . Do unto others as you would have them do unto you."

We must also take Jesus seriously when he says, "I am the way, the truth and the life, no one comes to the Father, but by me."

We believe that ultimate truth is found in the person of Jesus Christ. At the heart of the Christian faith there is a radical love but there is also a radical truth that we must hold onto.

That is the task of the local church anywhere it is located. As a local church in Utah, we have to figure out how we are going to respond to the challenge of the LDS Church. If all we do is emphasize love and getting along with our neighbors, the truth suffers. If we emphasize truth and only make it about pointing out the errors of Mormonism, it is easy for love and grace to be the casualty.

As I look at different churches and ministries in Utah, they tend to attract people with similar personalities. Some Christians are all about being right. They gravitate to churches that are all about truth. Some Christians are all about being liked, and so they gravitate to churches that are all about getting along. Local churches should not be about attracting people with similar personalities.

The only personality that should matter is the personality of Jesus. The Apostle John (the disciple that Jesus loved) said this about the personality of Jesus in John 1:14. Jesus was *full* of grace and *full* of truth.

Andy Stanley, in his book *Deep and Wide*, points out that John does not say that Jesus balanced truth and grace. He was full of both. The question is what does it look like to be full of grace and full of truth in a place like Utah?

Chapter 22
A New Perspective

How would Jesus shepherd a local church in a place like Utah? The culture of Utah is dominated by a people that belong to a rival religious faith and have had a history of antagonism with people like us, evangelical Christians.

Before we arrived in Utah, I sat down and read through the gospels and something jumped out at me: Jesus dealt with a people that were members of a rival religious faith and had a history of antagonism with his own people, the Jewish people. They were the Samaritans. Over the next several chapters, we are going to look at the interactions Jesus had with the Samaritans. As we do, a model emerges for local church ministry here in Utah.

The origins of the Samaritan people go back to the time when the nation of Israel was divided into two kingdoms. After the death of Solomon, the northern kingdom, Israel, divided from the southern kingdom, Judah. The great advantage of Judah was that Jerusalem was its capital and with that they had possession of the Temple. They were also led by kings who were descendants from the tribe of Judah and descendants of David.

Israel was made up of the northern tribes. Israel survived as a nation until 722 B.C. when Assyria defeated Israel and sent colonists to live and eventually intermarry with the people of Israel. Over time, a separate religious culture was born, which became the Samaritan people.

Jews did not accept Samaritans as true believers. Jews saw Samaritans as heretics and half-breeds. In time, the Samaritans developed their own version of the Torah, their own priesthood, their own temple. They claimed to be the one true faith of Yahweh. Samaritans and Jews became religious competitors. By the time Jesus arrived, the rift between Samaritan and Jew was huge. Samaritans were the competition.

So there is an analogy: Mormons are to evangelicals what Samaritans were to Jews. The question then is, "How does Jesus, a Jew, deal with the Samaritans, the religious competition?" Asking this question helped create a paradigm shift in the way we look at ministry to Mormons.

We came to realize that standing for truth is not just about winning the debate; it is not about just having the right information. It is also a matter of incarnation. The local church is called to not only communicate truth but to live it out in whatever context we find ourselves in. We came to see that Jesus has a lot to say to the local church in Utah through his interaction with Samaritans.

The first time we run across Samaritans in the gospels is in Luke 9:51-53. "As the time approached for him to be taken up to Heaven, Jesus resolutely set out for Jerusalem. He sent messengers on ahead, who went into a Samaritan village to get things ready for him; but the people there did not welcome him, because he was heading for Jerusalem."

In this passage, Jesus is in Galilee and is heading south with his disciples to Jerusalem. Samaria is between Galilee in the north and Judea in the South. When the Samaritan villagers realized that Jesus and his disciples were going to Jerusalem to worship, they would not allow them to stay in their village. They did not want to do anything which supported worship in the temple at Jerusalem. Jesus and His disciples received no hospitality from this Samaritan village.

Luke 9:54: "When the disciples James and John saw this, they asked, 'Lord, do you want us to call fire down from heaven to destroy them?'"

There you have what the average Jew at that time would see as the

132

answer to the Samaritan problem. The answer was a divine bombing run over this Samaritan village. I have noticed there are people who want to have a ministry to Mormons which employs the ministry methods of James and John. Ministry to Mormons can sometimes attract people who like to argue and who have a high need to be right.

Luke 9:55: "But Jesus turned and rebuked them." Jesus does not hate Samaritans. Jesus does not hate Mormons. He would rebuke anti-Mormonism. We're not here to attack the LDS people, we're here to reach them and to love them.

What does Jesus do? Luke 9:56: "And they went on to another village." Jesus does not argue. He does not state his reasons why Jerusalem and the temple were the true places of worship. He does not feed into the disciple's victim mentality. He does not recall other similar incidents where Samaritans had treated Jews poorly. He does not add fuel to the fire.

Jesus simply moved on. This is something I have badly needed to learn. I have, at times, wanted to respond the way that James and John did. Some of my biggest regrets have to do with my immediate reactions to perceived slights I have received from the LDS community. I have had moments where I have felt minimized, marginalized, and misunderstood in my interactions with LDS people.

It is actually a broader lesson than that. Sometimes within our ministry here at CenterPoint, I have had to learn to move on. The painful thing I have come to realize is that I don't like it when people do not see things my way. I want to try and convince people that I am right.

I have had so many incredible, life-giving relationships through the years. I have also been involved in a fair amount of conflict. One of my biggest regrets in ministry are all the times I have obsessed about conflict and spent sleepless nights wrestling with relationships where I have felt hurt. The words of Romans 12:18 are powerful: "If possible, as far as it depends on you, be at peace with all people." Sometimes when you have done what you can do, you need to learn to move on.

If you are heading anywhere in a purposeful manner, as Jesus was in his journey to Jerusalem, there will be resistance. There are times as a pastor when you need to speak to that resistance and communicate the values and vision of the church that you lead *for the sake of the church*. There are times I have needed to stand up and defend the ministry of the church which I lead.

There are times when you just need to move on. Jesus was able to move on because, in the end, he had a greater goal in mind. Jesus had set his face toward Jerusalem and the cross. We have a greater goal in mind than defending ourselves, and that is preaching the message of that cross.

Before we reach out to Mormons, we have to ask ourselves, "Why are we interested in reaching out to them? Why are we interested in growing a church at the center point of LDS culture? Are we motivated by a desire to win arguments and defeat our enemy, or do we sincerely love the LDS people?"

In the very next chapter in Luke 10:30-37, we once again see Jesus talking about Samaritans. This time, it is in one of his most memorable stories, the story of the Good Samaritan. In this story, a man is beaten and left half-dead on the road from Jerusalem to Jericho. The robbers have also stripped this man of his clothes so there is no way to identify whether he is a Jew or a Samaritan. A priest and a Levite walk by and do nothing to help the man. Then a Samaritan walks by and puts the man on his donkey and takes him to an inn where he can heal up.

To make it more real for someone like me, imagine Jesus telling the story this way. "A man traveling from Salt Lake to Orem was carjacked late one evening. His wallet was stolen. He was beaten badly and left half-dead. A pastor drove by and saw the man, but the board meeting that evening had gone late; he was tired, so he drove on home. Then a youth pastor drove by and saw the same man. He had an early morning meeting the next day, so he drove by as well. Then a Mormon came by and saw the man. He had compassion on him, applied first aid, put him in his car, and took him to the hospital. Which of these three men was his neighbor?"

When I tell the story that way, I get an idea of how the Jews listening to the story of the Good Samaritan might have felt. They had to wonder "Why would Jesus make our competition the example of what it meant to be a good neighbor?" Was Jesus saying that Samaritans were superior to Jews? Are Mormons superior to evangelical Christians? I don't believe that is the point of the story.

So often, we hear stories of what good people the Mormons are. We hear about all sorts of things Mormons do, things we ought to be doing. Having lived among Mormons for 30 years, I find they have a lot of admirable traits. Mormons often make great neighbors. They are often willing to help people in need. At the same time, Mormons are people, just like us. I don't believe the point of this story is for us to try to be more like any one group of people like the Mormons.

Jesus is saying something to his Jewish brethren. Jews believed that the Samaritans were the problem. For a lot of modern-day disciples of Jesus who are living in Utah, it is easy to believe that Mormons are the problem. The great lesson I have had to learn in living here is that my Mormon neighbors are not the problem. My problem is me and the attitude I choose to live with in this place.

The great challenge here is not to be like the Mormons; the great challenge is to be like Jesus. The great challenge is to truly love our neighbors.

Jesus is asking me a simple question through this story: "Am I a neighbor to the people I live around? Are we loving people here the way Jesus would love them?"

The question for us is "How would Jesus love Samaritans?"

The answer to that question tells me a lot about what it looks like to live in this place and lead a church which seeks to reach the people who live here.

Chapter 23
Show Up

There are answers to the question "How would Jesus love Samaritans?" They are found in John 4, where we see Jesus taking a different trip through Samaria. John 4:4: "Now he had to go through Samaria." On this occasion, Jesus is in Judea and is headed to Galilee. Again, Judea is in the south and Galilee is in the north, and it says he had to go through Samaria.

He actually did not *have* to go through Samaria. Many devout Jews would take a more circuitous route around Samaria in order to avoid being defiled by coming into contact with Samaritans. Jesus showed up in Samaria on purpose. He shows up because he has good news for the Samaritan people.

The way Jesus shows up in the gospels is in person, in bodily form. How does Jesus show up today? Jesus shows up today through his body, the church. Jesus wants His church to show up in places like Utah. As Jesus shows up in John 4, he has a lot to say to us about what the ministry of a local church looks like in a place like Utah.

Before we talk about the church in Utah, I want to make an observation about evangelical Christians and the way we talk about the church. We love to talk about the church in an abstract way. We like talking about the "Universal Church" or, as some call it, the "Invisible Church." It is called the *universal church* because it exists in Heaven and on Earth and it is made up of everyone who belongs to Jesus by faith. This is the church that Jesus speaks of in Matthew 16:18 when he says, "I will build my church . . ." It is called "invisible" because only God knows who truly belongs to it.

The New Testament also talks about the local church, or the visible church. The local church is located in specific places all around the world. The local church is where people show up week-in and week-out for worship and fellowship. This is where people grow up into maturity in the family of God. This is where we fellowship, serve, and give. The local church is called to take the good news into the culture it is located in.

I believe that reaching the people of Utah comes down to the health of the local church in Utah. In 1989, there were not a lot of us. Back then, when I would travel outside of Utah and tell people that I was a pastor in Utah, I would often hear people say, "Utah, and all those Mormons? How could anyone live there?"

Things have changed. Today, there is something of a church-planting movement in Utah. It has become more and more common for churches and denominations to plant churches in Utah. I am grateful for it.

I have had a number of opportunities to talk to church planters who want to know the secret sauce for growing a healthy church in Utah. My response is "Show up, and then keep on showing up."

Another way I say it is "If you are going to come here, then buy a burial plot." Don't look at this as a stepping-stone to something bigger and better someplace else. Come here to stay, and if that sounds like a life sentence, this may not be a great fit.

The reason I say that is because a church in Utah that leads people to the Jesus of the Bible is going to face opposition. Sometimes, that opposition is going to seem spiritual in nature. Leaders of churches experience spiritual oppression here. I am by nature a positive, optimistic person. But there are times when I have sunk into depression and despair. The Devil has a message for us in moments like that: "Right now would be a really good time to hang it up and leave."

How do we respond in those moments? The simple answer is that we need to pray. Prayer is not my natural response when I am struggling. My natural response is to try harder, to do something, anything. So often I have been led to the place where all of my resources and efforts have been exhausted. Jesus has often brought me to places where all I have left to do is pray.

I do believe that God answers prayer in specific ways. Prayer changes things, but prayer also changes us. Somehow, through prayer, I am led to see our church and this ministry the way Jesus sees it. So often the objective evidence seems to point to a place where we believe we are losing.

Jesus changes my perspective to see that the battle is not *against* the people we live around. It is *for* them. Ephesians 6:12: "For our struggle is not against flesh and blood, but against the rulers, against the authorities, against the powers of this dark world, and against the spiritual forces of evil in the heavenly realms."

In so many ways through the years, I see Jesus on the move, changing lives. I am able to see that not only is Jesus winning but that he has won. I learn through prayer to leave the results to Him and to stay faithful and keep showing up.

There is another piece of advice I give people who have shown up to plant churches or pastor already existing churches in Utah: "Stay focused."

It is amazing to me the number of "ministry opportunities" that come our direction. Evangelical Christians have lots of great ideas. We are great at starting things. Sometimes people see our church and whatever resources we have and think, "Think of what we could do if we could get these people behind the ministry I want to start." If you start buying into every idea that comes your way, then pretty soon you get distracted from your primary purpose.

I am for whatever advances the cause of the local church in the state of Utah.

I believe that there are all sorts of things we can do to partner with other churches and other ministries which contribute to the health of the local church in Utah. As the shepherd of this church, I am not responsible for other churches and ministries. I am responsible for this flock and its health.

Whenever someone comes to me with a great ministry opportunity, I always have the same question: "How does this advance the cause of this local church?" I know this can sound selfish. I care about other ministries in Utah. I care deeply. But I am not the shepherd of all the churches in Utah. I am called to lead this local church.

Jesus did not say "yes" to everything he was asked to do. Jesus did not say "yes" to every ministry opportunity that came his way. In Luke 12, when a man came and said, "Tell my brother to divide the inheritance with me," Jesus declined to be the arbiter between these two men.

Jesus did not heal everyone. In John 5, at the pool of Bethesda, there were many who needed healing on that day when Jesus showed up. On that day, Jesus appears to have healed only one man among the many who needed healing. Jesus did not "disciple" everyone. He only had 12 disciples, and of those 12, it is pretty clear that he gave three more attention than the others. He was focused.

Evangelical Christianity, as a movement, is filled with all sorts of organizations and people with vision and great ideas. The weakness of our movement is that we have failed to focus on the main idea that Jesus had— that is, the local church. If we, as shepherds of local churches in Utah, say yes to every "opportunity," we might never get around to the main thing we have been called to do: to shepherd the flock of God.

Chapter 24
Settle Down

John 4:4: "So he came to a town in Samaria called Sychar, near the plot of ground Jacob had given to his son Joseph. Jacob's well was there, and Jesus, tired as he was from the journey, sat down by the well."

Jesus is not just in foreign territory as he shows up at Jacob's Well. He is truly at the center point of Samaritan culture. Jacob's Well was the most revered place for the Samaritan people. The Jews might have the temple in Jerusalem, but they were in possession of the well that had belonged to the father of the nation, Jacob, aka Israel. As Samaritans came to this well to draw water, they did so with the awareness that they were connected to the father of the nation of Israel.

As Jesus, a Jew, shows up at Jacob's Well, he is the ultimate outsider. It is important to see that he "sat down." You could say that he made himself at home. He relaxed. We need to do the same here in Utah. We realize in coming to this place that we do so as outsiders. We need to settle down, make ourselves at home, and, in a way, act like we belong here.

That sense of belonging the Mormon people have is greater than just a lot of people belonging to the same church. So often the families we seek to reach have large, extended families living in the area. Along with that, these families have strong generational ties to this place. Many of the families here are descendants of pioneer stock. They have a sense of belonging because their ancestors have a history here. The reality is that we are not a part of that.

That sense of not belonging and isolation outsiders experience is heightened by the fact that everyone else seems so connected. The LDS Church organizes its congregations geographically. When you live in Utah, you are very aware that you live within the boundaries of a ward (an LDS congregation). That means that everyone within those boundaries shows up at the same church on Sunday mornings.

When we moved to Provo, out of forty homes in the neighborhood that we lived in, we were the only non-LDS family. Our church service times would often coincide with the starting times in the local ward. As I would leave our neighborhood, I would often find myself in a line of cars leaving our neighborhood for church. But as everyone else turned left into the ward parking lot, my car continued on up the road to our church in Orem. I sometimes felt like the missing man in a Blue Angels flight formation.

After about five years living in our neighborhood, a new guy moved in across the street. I saw him on a Sunday, and I walked over to shake his hand and introduce myself.

He told me his name was Al and that he had just moved from California. He then looked at me and said, "I didn't see you at church today."

I said, "Well, there's a reason for that. I am the Pastor at a church up in Orem."

Then he said, "Oh! I hope you feel welcome!"

I said, "Al, I have lived here in this neighborhood for five years and you haven't been here a week, and you are the one that is welcoming me. Shouldn't I be the one welcoming you?"

We both knew the reason for that. No matter how long he lived here, he belonged because he was Mormon. At the time it felt like no matter how long I lived here, without becoming Mormon, I would never truly belong.

The problem with living at the center point of Mormon culture is that it forces you to define yourself in terms of Mormonism. You are either a Mormon, a non-Mormon, a "jack" Mormon (a term for an inactive Mormon), an anti-Mormon, or an ex-Mormon.

Back in the mid-90s, I was asked to speak to the Chamber of Commerce. *Money Magazine* had just named Provo the number one "most livable city" in the United States. After the article was published, the Chamber of Commerce was getting calls from people outside the area saying, "We are thinking about moving to Utah Valley, but we are not Mormons, is that okay?"

That was the topic I was given to speak on. The way I answered the question was to say, "I love Provo-Orem. I hope to live here for the rest of my life. This is a wonderful place to live. There is a problem, though. Look at how you asked the question, 'I am not a Mormon, is that okay?' It's not okay because you're asking me to define myself by what I'm not, rather than what I am. I am not a non-Mormon. I'm a follower of Jesus. I am a Christian. I want to live that way around you."

In moving to Utah, it was more than just me being an outsider from California. I was the pastor of an evangelical Christian church. People may not have said it, but there was a sense in which I was perceived to be a threat to their way of life.

How do you settle down and make yourself at home? By loving the people who live here. One way that we love the people here is to love what they love. People here love their kids. One practical way that I loved my neighbors' kids was by coaching my children's sports teams—everything from softball to soccer to baseball to football. When people see you loving their kids, it breaks down barriers.

Then there are those moments that are unforeseen. A few years after we moved into our neighborhood, a nine-year-old boy was killed in our neighborhood when he was run over by a garbage truck. It was awful. A number of children in the neighborhood saw it happen, and the neighborhood was in shock. We knew this family and knew this boy.

As people wandered around, I took a risk and gathered people together and I asked if we could pray. We gathered around and joined hands, and I prayed. A few days later, I got a letter from a neighbor. She said that people up until that moment did not know what to make of me but "now we know that you love us."

Nothing happens in this place if the people here do not believe that we love them.

Chapter 25
Reach Out

John 4:6b-7a: "It was about the sixth hour when a Samaritan woman came to draw water." One question that I am often asked by people interested in ministry in Utah is, "Who are we targeting?"

Who are we trying to reach?

Any church should look at their surroundings before they answer that question. We look at Utah Valley University, which is a half-mile down the road from our location, and BYU, which is less than four miles away. The combined 70,000 students who attend these universities would tell us that we ought to be trying to reach college students. We also live in a valley of 600,000 people, where there are 130,000 K-12 students. We are trying to reach families with children.

There is another answer. We reach out to whoever shows up in our lives. This woman shows up at noon while Jesus is sitting at the well. This was not the normal time for someone to show up and draw water. The sixth hour was high noon, the heat of the day. Women in that culture would show up at the well at the beginning of the day when it was cool to draw their water. As they filled up their jars, they would greet one another and share what was going on in their lives.

This woman comes out at noon for a reason. This is the time that she would be least likely to run into anyone else. As we shall see, she has some things going on in her life that she would rather not talk about. She has a checkered past. She has been married five times, and the man she is living with now is not her husband. She comes alone because she does not want to be stared at and whispered about. She is tired of being judged.

The last person in the world she thought she would end up talking to when she left her house that day was a Jewish rabbi. Jesus reaches out to this woman. He does so by making a simple request of her: "Will you give me a drink?"

As insignificant and as ordinary as this request seems to be, there is actually a lot to learn from this moment. Jesus understood the importance of the ordinary. God does extraordinary things through the mundane, everyday happenings that go on in our lives.

This is something that evangelicals have a hard time understanding. We are all about the "big event." I have been a part of some big events here in Utah. In our early years here, we would often hear people say, "We need to bring Billy Graham to Utah. If we could just have Billy Graham come and draw a stadium filled with Mormons, Utah would be evangelized."

Billy Graham did not come to Utah. The fact is that lots of Mormons would listen to Billy Graham and have no problem with what he had to say.

In 1997, churches in Utah did come together for an evangelistic campaign called Utah Alive. The campaign brought out a British evangelist named John Guest. We rented the Huntsman Center at the University of Utah that seats 15,000 people. We were organized and well financed. John Guest was an incredible communicator (the British accent always helps). We had country music star Charlie Daniels come out one night to sing.

Although I don't remember the exact numbers of those in attendance, the place seemed kind of empty. I was the emcee of the event. I remember saying to myself night after night, "People are staying away in droves."

No doubt there were some good things that happened through the event. But it did not have the desired outcome we wanted it to have. We wanted to do something that reached significant numbers of Mormons. That did not happen.

Through this experience, I came to realize that Mormons are resistant to anything that is designed to target them. One of the reasons Mormons are resistant to a lot of traditional methods of evangelism is that Mormons themselves are an evangelistic people. Mormons know all about making people into projects. They smell it from a long way off, and they avoid it.

The things that make a difference in Utah are not the big events but the little ones. I am talking about the ordinary things that occur when Christ followers live in neighborhoods, go to work, and live their lives among people. Those little events happen as you sit with your neighbors at athletic events, concerts, and at picnics. It means getting to know people and getting involved in their lives.

However, we have found there is one "big event" that our neighbors are open to being invited to. After we have gotten to know them, we have found that Mormons are open to coming to a Sunday morning worship service at our church. Mormons are open to that because that is something we do as a part of our normal everyday lives. They are curious about what we do when we gather together.

When we invite people, we do so from the perspective that the church is a family. Like any family, we want to get to know our neighbors, and what better way to do that than to invite them over to our house?

We have also found that there are special times of the year, like Christmas, when our neighbors are open to coming to our church. Christmas is a big deal in Utah. We have a Christmas Eve service where almost half of the people that come are our LDS neighbors. At the same time, we also realize that our LDS neighbors are going to invite us to special events at their church. When we can, we go.

Some people have questioned our willingness to visit LDS church services. The question gets asked, "Aren't you legitimizing them as a church by doing so?"

No, I am simply loving my neighbor as myself. The golden rule comes into play here: "Do unto others as you would have them do unto you." Treat others the way that we want to be treated. If we would like our LDS neighbors to come and visit our services, how can we say, "I'm sorry, it is against my religion to visit yours."

Jesus asking this woman for a drink shows us something else: Jesus is authentic. He is thirsty. It is part of being a human being. Jesus and this woman are at that well for the same reason. They are both thirsty. In asking her for a drink, he builds a bridge to this woman.

People are longing for authenticity. Jesus is keeping it real. Authenticity is refreshing wherever it is found, especially in a culture like this. When people live in a close-knit religious community, they have the sense that they are constantly being watched and evaluated by what they eat and drink, what they wear, and how they talk.

One of the things we like to say is, "We are not trying to reach the un-churched, we are trying to reach the overly churched."

Often, the people we reach have come out of Mormonism and are, in many ways, sick of trying to keep up appearances. I believe that one of the ways we make a difference in the lives of our neighbors is to be honest about our own struggles, our own problems, and needs. When we are authentic, it gives people permission to be real with us.

This extends to what we do on Sunday mornings. One thing I have noticed about speakers in LDS services is that often they will speak with a different tone and cadence than everyday life. When we teach at CenterPoint, we want to talk to people the same way we talk to them the rest of the week. A sense of humor is important. The safest kind of humor is self-deprecating humor. People respond when we are able to laugh at ourselves.

This Samaritan woman in John 4 is actually shocked when Jesus asks her for a drink. She says, "You're a Jew, I'm a Samaritan woman, how can you ask me for a drink? For Jews do not associate with Samaritans."

Literally, that means that Jews and Samaritans do not drink from the same cup. To pious Jews, to drink from the same cup as a Samaritan woman meant defiling yourself.

One thing she was sure of was that this is not normal behavior for Jewish rabbis. Your typical Jewish rabbi would never be found talking to a woman like her at a place like Jacob's Well. Jesus never seemed to do what people expected him to. Jesus was not trying to live up to her stereotypes of a Jewish rabbi.

Mormons have stereotypes when it comes to pastors of non-LDS churches. The idea that a lot of LDS have of pastors it that of a pompous "know it all" impressed with their title and position. Beyond that, many LDS folk have the idea that we only do what we do because we collect a salary as pastors. The LDS Church does not pay their bishops.

There is not a lot I can do about people's ideas about what might be motivating me as a pastor. The one thing that I have tried to do through the years is to not play to the stereotypes.

In the early 2000s, I coached the ninth-grade football team at Orem High School across the street from our old church location. I didn't tell the kids or parents that I was a pastor. I wanted them to get to know me as a man and a coach before they saw me as a reverend or a pastor. People were shocked when they found out what my "real job" was. My hope was that those kids and their parents would go away from that experience knowing that I loved them.

Years ago, our next-door neighbor's daughter was getting married. I am not sure why she and her fiancé weren't getting married in the temple. They did have some connections, though, so they got married in the conference room of the Joseph Smith Building at Temple Square in Salt Lake City. It was as close to the temple as you could get without getting married in the temple. They asked me to marry them, and I said yes.

I wanted to ask, "Why are you asking me?" I don't think they had ever visited our church. All we had done was just lived our lives next to these people. They knew that we loved them.

Lots of ordinary things led to something that was kind of out of the ordinary. When I stood up in front with the bride and groom at the Joseph Smith Building and told people I was the pastor of a church down in Orem, mouths dropped open all over the room. On that occasion, I had an opportunity to share some good news in a place I never imagined I would be invited to go.

These were incredible experiences. They occurred because we were different than what they thought we were going to be. The biggest stereotype of all that Mormons have is that pastors and the congregations they lead do not like Mormons. I want to live in a way that disproves that stereotype.

Chapter 26
Good News

Jesus has shown up in Samaria because he loves the Samaritan people and he has good news for them. The woman Jesus meets at the well has a hard time believing that. She is immediately defensive. "You are a Jew and I am a Samaritan woman, how can you ask me for a drink?" (John 4:9) Jesus could have responded to her defensiveness by taking the opportunity to enter into a discussion on the finer points of Samaritan and Jewish theology. He could have come up with a list of offenses that Samaritans had committed toward the Jews.

It is really easy living here to get into a debate about any number of subjects along the Mormon/evangelical divide. But beginning the conversation with an attack is a good way to keep people from ever listening to the gospel.

Rather than attacking Samaritanism, Jesus begins with the good news about Himself. John 4:10: "Jesus answered her, 'If you knew the gift of God and who it is that asks you for a drink, you would have asked Him, and He would have given you living water.'" Notice that Jesus has said nothing about Samaritans and Jews.

When you start a relationship with all that is wrong with Mormonism, Mormons easily see it as an attack. When people are attacked, they resist. When people resist, it has a way of strengthening their resolve to remain what they are. It has a way of confirming their beliefs. Even if you convince them they are wrong, what is the outcome?

I had a Latter-day Saint guy once say to me, "If you were to attack my faith and sink this boat that I have been sailing on my entire life and leave me floating out in the water, I am not sure that I would want to climb on your boat even if you were to throw me a life preserver."

This woman's greatest problem was not that she was a Samaritan. Her greatest problem was that her soul was as dry and parched as her tongue. Jesus does not see her as a Samaritan woman but as a human being. This is the most basic way that we relate to others. Jesus did not see her ethnicity, her gender, her nationality, or her religion. He saw a human being created in the image of God. His goal was to bring her life, to give her living water.

I have met a number of evangelicals who believe that if you are for the people that live here, you are compromising. I have taken a lot from Jeremiah 29 in that regard. In that chapter, Jeremiah writes a letter to the Jewish exiles in Babylon. They are in a place they do not want to be in. These exiles desperately wanted to go home to Jerusalem, but Jeremiah told them to make a home there . . . in Babylon.

He said (Jeremiah 29:5-7), "Seek the peace and prosperity of the city to which I have carried you into exile. Pray to the Lord for it, because if it prospers, you too will prosper."

Historically, we know that in Babylon, the Jews maintained the beliefs and practices, which allowed them to remain a distinct people. Part of their identity in Babylon was that they were *for* the peace and prosperity of the city. As Professor Harold Netland of Trinity Evangelical Divinity School puts it, "They adopted a positive attitude and acted intentionally to pursue the wellbeing of the city."

Make no mistake, Babylon had a plan for the Jewish people. Babylon wanted the Jews to assimilate and lose their identity. God also had a plan. God wanted to use the Jewish presence in Babylon to assimilate Babylonians into his kingdom.

When it comes to CenterPoint Church, there are times when it seems like we are a church filled with exiles. We have lots of people who would rather be someplace else. God calls us to seek the peace and prosperity of the place to which we have been called: Utah Valley. If this place prospers, so do we, and so does the gospel.

What are some ways we can be for people? When I got here in 1989, I started praying for the BYU football team. I had been a high school football coach in California. I love the game and have always loved working with football players and coaches. Major college football programs necessarily have to build some walls around their programs to protect their players and coaches. I realized that if anything were ever going to happen, it would have to begin on the inside. We had players who were on the team who would come to the church. I would pray for these guys.

I started praying for something else. BYU has hired non-LDS football coaches through the years. I started praying they would hire someone who would see this as an opportunity for ministry.

In 2003, a new offensive line coach was hired at BYU by the name of Jeff Grimes. Jeff and his wife, Sheri, started attending our church. Jeff was not just a coach who happened to be a Christian. He was a Christian who happened to be a football coach.

In the first year Jeff was there, the head coach of the BYU football team realized there was a need among the non-LDS guys on the team for some spiritual direction. Jeff said, "I will get my pastor to come and do a Bible study."

We began to do a Bible study with non-LDS members of the BYU football team. Jeff and Sheri moved on after three years but have become some of our closest friends through the years.

Even though we no longer have the same Bible study going with the team, we continue to have a ministry with the football team. Not everyone in our church has taken it kindly when I talk about supporting BYU football. I have had people say, "How can you be for a football team that represents the LDS Church?"

My support of the BYU football team has nothing to do with the LDS Church. It has to do with the people involved in the program. Through the years, I have grown to love the coaches and the guys on the football team, and I am for them. It is amazing what happens when people know that you are for them.

Keeping it about the good news does not mean it is easy. There is a huge barrier when it comes to communicating the good news to the LDS people. You see it in this woman's response to the offer that Jesus has made her of living water. John 4:11: "The woman said, 'You have nothing to draw with and the well is deep. Where can you get this living water?'"

This woman can only think in terms of drinking water. Her response to Jesus is the water he seeks to bring her cannot be from this well because the well is deep, and Jesus has brought nothing to draw with. So where is Jesus going to find this living water? She asks in John 4:12, "Are you greater than our father Jacob, who gave us the well and drank from it himself, as did also his sons and his livestock?"

Her question to Jesus is really "Are you saying that your Jewish water is better than our Samaritan water? Do you think that you are greater than our father Jacob who drew from this well himself?" She is very much in the mindset of "We Samaritans have something that you Jews do not have. We have this well. How could you possibly have water that would be superior to this water?"

Sometimes in our conversations with Mormons, we see the same thing. Mormons have the mindset of "Look at our church with its wealth, organization, and expansion. How could you possibly have anything which compares to this?"

The discussion seems to center around the question, "Whose church is better, mine or yours?"

If it was a matter of which church is the wealthiest and best organized, then you would have to give the LDS Church serious consideration. Jesus did not come to this earth to set up the perfect church organization. He came to seek and to save the lost. This woman was lost. That is why Jesus resists making the discussion about Samaritans and Jews.

Jesus says, "Everyone who drinks this water will be thirsty again, but whoever drinks the water I give them will never thirst. Indeed, the water I give them will become in them a spring of water welling up to eternal life." (John 4:13-14)

Jesus once again addresses the real spiritual need that exists in the woman's life. She responds by saying (John 4:15), "Sir, give me this water so that I won't get thirsty and have to keep coming here to draw water."

It is now clear that this woman and Jesus have been using the same words but are giving those words different definitions. Jesus is talking about living (spiritual) water, and she is talking about drinking water (H_2O). This is similar to the problem we have as we seek to communicate the good news to Mormon people. We have a vocabulary such that we share all sorts of "faith words" but we give those words different definitions. The reason for this is that we have different sources of authority. In a sense, we are working from different dictionaries.

Evangelicals look to the Bible as our sole source of authority. Latter-day Saints believe in the Bible but will say, "We have more." They believe they are the restoration of the one true church with a living prophet, the restored priesthood, and along with that, added scripture. They claim to possess a unique and exclusive spiritual authority no one else has.

Because we have different sources of authority, we have ended up with very different worldviews. It seems this is where a lot of our conversations with Latter-day Saints end up bogging down. We have these conversations about God, sin, salvation, the church, and Jesus, and we end up getting nowhere because we are defining those words based on our very different views of authority.

It is at this point that it would seem it might be a good time to end the conversation. Jesus doesn't stop there. He asks a telling question.

Chapter 27
The Heart of the Matter

John 4:16-18: "He told her, 'Go, call your husband and come back.'" Jesus makes a simple request of this woman to go get her husband. She is guarded in her response: "'I have no husband,' she replied.".

As we are about to see, it is just a small part of the truth about what is really going on in her life. Up to this point, Jesus has presented this woman with a compelling message. She has come out to the well because she is thirsty. We all are. We cannot live without water. Her physical thirst is a spot-on picture of her spiritual life. Her need for "living water" ought to be apparent, but the words of Jesus make no sense to her.

By asking her to go and get her husband, Jesus has asked the one question that makes her think about all that is wrong with her life. She is a moral and a religious failure. She is a social outcast. This simple request to go and get her husband had to bring all of that to mind. Her life is a mess.

"Jesus said to her, 'You are right when you say you have no husband. The fact is, you have had five husbands, and the man you now have is not your husband. What you have just said is quite true.'" This Jewish rabbi has seen her and knows all about her life. She has been through a series of failed relationships, and that failure has led her to this moment where she now has to come out to the well at noon to avoid contact with the rest of her community.

This is a painful moment, but painfully good. There is something in all of us that wants to avoid being found out. There is also something in us that is dying to find someone and someplace where we can be real. Jesus is saying that "there is a place where you can get real, where you no longer have to hide, it is in my presence."

This is really what the local church at its best is all about. The way Jesus is present in the world today is through his body, the Church. Jesus wants His church to be a place where people can come and find Him and when they do, to be honest about where they really are in life.

The people making this journey out of Mormonism have pretty much had it with organized religion. But there is something about Jesus that draws them. Jesus doesn't love us once we get ourselves all cleaned up. "While we were yet sinners, Jesus dies for us." He doesn't love the image we try to create. He loves us, just as we are, broken life and all.

When I meet people on this journey out of the LDS Church, sometimes they wonder why I would ever want to pastor in a place like this. The reason I have stayed and continued to do what I do is *not* so we can continue to hold religious services and "do church."

In those times when I have thought, "Right now would be a good time to hang it up," the thing that has kept me going is I never get tired of people like this woman coming to Jesus and finding life.

One thing that speaks to me in this passage is that up to this point, Jesus has given this Samaritan woman a brilliant presentation of the good news. His message has fallen on deaf ears. I have had a lot of opportunities to share the good news with Mormon people in my time here in Utah. I have preached thousands of sermons. There have been messages I have been really excited about that seemed like they would make so much sense to someone from an LDS background. Often, it seems my words fall on deaf ears.

This passage teaches us that if people do not see their need, then the gospel message, no matter how well it is articulated, will make no sense. We have to be comfortable with the reality that we are going to meet people throughout our lives who are not ready to hear. At the same time,

I can also say there have been times when the Lord has used my most inadequate efforts to change lives. When the Holy Spirit is working in people's lives to convince them of their need for Jesus, people listen. Our task is to be sensitive to where God is working.

The first year I was here, I would get our bulletin for our Sunday services ready and then go to a copy shop to make copies. A young guy who worked there would run them off for me. Every week, he would look at the bulletin and make comments on whatever it was I was going to speak on the next Sunday. Sometimes, those comments led to longer discussions.

I tried to keep it positive, but these often led to what he called our "weekly Bible bashes." These were mini debates. No matter how much sense I thought I was making, my words made no impact on my copy shop friend. I was actually kind of glad when we got our own copy machine because he was wearing me out. After that, I lost contact with him.

Almost thirty years later, a BYU student came to me. She was attending our church and was in the process of leaving the LDS Church. She told me her dad knew me. Her dad was my buddy from the copy shop. A few months later, he showed up at church. He had been through a divorce. He was newly remarried. He was in an entirely different place. He was open. Life and the Holy Spirit have a way of doing that to you.

I don't care where you go, people are broken. People in this culture are broken by failure, by the expectations of their religion, by their own guilt and shame. They (and we) are drawn to Jesus because when you meet Him, there is something in us that senses He can make us whole.

It says something about this woman that she stays around even after Jesus lays the hard truth about her life before her. She does not at first want to talk about her broken life. She has questions about where you find the truth.

She says (John 4:19-20), "I can see that you are a prophet. Our fathers worshiped on this mountain, but you Jews claim that the place where we must worship is in Jerusalem."

Notice the pronouns. She begins by talking about "our fathers." She may be a total failure as a Samaritan, but she is still a Samaritan. To her, it all comes down to this question, "Who has the one true religion? Jews or Samaritans?"

It is important to see here that it is the woman and not Jesus who brings up the religious conflict between Jews and Samaritans. No one could have accused Jesus of being anti-Samaritan. Throughout the conversation, Jesus has been talking to her about a relationship with God, but she is the one who wants to talk about their respective religions.

She is actually asking the question of authority: "Who is right when it comes to answering the question of where we find the one true place of worship? Is it you Jews, or is it our Samaritan fathers?"

Both Jews and Samaritans believed themselves to be the one true religion. Jews said that God must be worshiped in Jerusalem. The reason the Jews said that was because Jerusalem was where the temple was located. That was where Jews said there was an authentic priesthood that performed rituals that brought people into relationship with God.

The Samaritans also had such a place. They said God was to be worshiped at Mount Gerizim. Samaritans also claimed to have their own priesthood that performed similar rituals. So, who is right? Who is it that has authority to act and speak for God?

The question we get asked so often here in Utah is similar. "Where do I find the one true church?"

That question is related to another question: "Where do you get your authority? What qualifies you to speak and act on behalf of God?"

Mormons believe Jesus has restored the one true church through Joseph Smith and now the Church of Jesus Christ of Latter-day Saints alone, headquartered in Salt Lake City, has the authority to not only speak for God but to perform ordinances that save and exalt.

When I meet Mormon people who sincerely care about me, they wonder how I cannot see the simple truth of that. At some point in the relationship, we do need to talk about truth. As Peter says in 1 Peter 3:16: "Always be prepared to give an answer to everyone who asks you to give the reason for the hope that you have. But do this with gentleness and respect."

Chapter 28
Answering the Golden Questions

Mormons are encouraged to ask their neighbors and friends what they call "the golden questions." Those questions are, "What do you know about the Church of Jesus Christ of Latter-day Saints?" and "Would you like to know more?"

Mormons usually don't ask me the golden questions because after you live here as long as I have, they realize I might already know some things about the LDS Church.

The question people ask me is, "How come you are not a Mormon?" When I get asked this question, my usual response is to say, "Do you really want to have this conversation? Because it is a hard one to have."

What makes it a difficult conversation is not that I am going to tell them about all of the problems I have had living around Mormons. That is clearly not the case, as I hope I have made clear I have loved living around the LDS people. The reason it is a difficult conversation is because whether or not the Church of Jesus Christ of Latter-day Saints is true comes down to the Book of Mormon and Joseph Smith.

If the Book of Mormon is true, then Joseph Smith is a prophet and the church that he founded is true. The reason it is a difficult conversation is that I do not believe in a book Mormons believe is scripture. I do not believe that the man who brought us that book is a prophet.

It is hard to overestimate the importance of the Book of Mormon to the LDS Church. When we arrived in Utah in 1989, Ezra Taft Benson was president of the LDS Church.

President Benson clearly saw the centrality of the Book of Mormon to the LDS Church. He said, "Take away the book of Mormon and the revelations, and where is our religion? We have none."

He understood that the LDS Church does not exist apart from the Book of Mormon. That is why his charge to LDS missionaries was to "flood the earth with the Book of Mormon."

The LDS Church makes huge claims about the Book of Mormon. Joseph Smith said, "I told the brethren that 'the Book of Mormon was the most correct of any book on earth, and the keystone of our religion, and a man would get nearer to God by abiding by its precepts than by any other book.'" (History of the Church, 4:461.)

Why don't I believe in the Book of Mormon? There are several reasons. One of the first is that in the preface to the Book of Mormon it says that this book "contains the fullness of the everlasting gospel."

Despite its claim to contain the fullness of the everlasting gospel, the Book of Mormon simply does not teach a lot of what happens in Mormonism as it is practiced in the LDS Church.

For example, in the Book of Mormon, there's nothing about a restored priesthood. There's nothing about celestial marriage, the Word of Wisdom, the preexistence, baptism for the dead, temple work, or church organizational structure. If this book contains the fullness of the gospel, then where are those things that are so essential to the LDS faith?

One of the compelling ideas that attracted people to the Book of Mormon and Mormonism in the early years of the faith is that when it was produced, there seemed to be all of these competing ideas about the true nature of Christianity among the different sects and denominations of Christianity. Mormon missionaries made the claim that the Book of Mormon clarified those issues and settled those disputes.

Mormon missionaries used to use an illustration where they would say, "Imagine a Bible nailed onto a table. Once you drive that one nail through it, you can turn it any way you want." Mormonism presupposes the Bible is deficient and corrupted and can be interpreted in any number of ways.

Then they would say that if you take a Book of Mormon and lay it on top of the Bible and drive a nail in the two books together, those books can no longer be turned and twisted. The idea is that the Book of Mormon fixes interpretation and settles all doctrinal controversies that have divided Christians.

The Book of Mormon does not settle doctrinal controversies. In fact, the Book of Mormon teaches things that Mormons do not believe. Take the doctrine of God. There is nothing in the Book of Mormon about eternal progression and God being an exalted man. It actually says just the opposite. Moroni 8:18 says, "I know that God is not a partial God, neither a changeable being, but he is unchangeable from all eternity."

The far bigger problem with the Book of Mormon is not in what it does or does not teach. The greater issue is that it claims to be a historical record of people who actually lived in this hemisphere. Once again, the preface to the Book of Mormon says, "The Book of Mormon is a volume of holy scripture comparable to the Bible. It is a record of God's dealings with ancient inhabitants of the Americas and contains the fulness of the everlasting gospel."

LDS leaders know what is at stake in making this claim. On the official website of the LDS Church, we have Apostle Jeffrey Holland making the following statement: "Everything in the Church—everything—rises or falls on the truthfulness of the Book of Mormon and, by implication, the Prophet Joseph Smith's account of how it came forth . . . It sounds like a 'sudden death' proposition to me. Either the Book of Mormon is what the Prophet Joseph said it is, or this Church and its founder are false, fraudulent, a deception from the first instance onward." (Excerpted from a Church Educational System Religious Educators' Symposium address given at Brigham Young University on August 9, 1994)

From the very beginning, a claim is made that this is a history of a real people who lived in a real time and a real place. J. Reuben Clark, for whom the BYU law school was named, stated, "If we have the truth, it cannot be harmed by investigation. If we have not the truth, it ought to be harmed."

In that spirit, let's look at the question, "Is there any real evidence that the things contained in the Book of Mormon really happened?"

The Book of Mormon story begins around 600 BC with the story of Lehi, an Israelite who leaves Jerusalem with his family and travels over the ocean and lands someplace in the Americas. Lehi has two sons, Laman and Nephi. The descendants of Nephi are righteous. The Lamanites were wicked.

We are told in 2 Nephi 5:21 that because of their iniquity there was a curse put upon them "wherefore, as they were white, and exceedingly fair and delightsome, that they might not be enticing unto my people the Lord God did cause a skin of blackness to come upon them." These two peoples became identifiable because of their skin color.

There are wars fought between these two peoples until the Lamanites wipe out the Nephites. This is the Book of Mormon's explanation of where the Native Americans came from. They are the Lamanites. They are actual descendants of Israel.

When we first arrived in Utah, it was common to hear Mormons refer to Native Americans by their Book of Mormon name, "Lamanites." There was even a BYU performance group made up of Native Americans called The Lamanite Generation.

I have not heard the term Lamanite in quite a while, though. The name Lamanite draws attention to the Mormon view of the Israelite origins of Native Americans. The problem is that we now know Native Americans are not Israelite or Semitic in origin. DNA samples have been taken from Native American tribes throughout North and South America. There's not a trace of submitted DNA in any of the Native Americans which is Israelite or Semitic. It is almost all from Asia.

The LDS Church has recognized this as a problem. The introduction to the Book of Mormon used to say that the Lamanites are "the principle ancestors of the American Indians." In 2007, the LDS Church changed the statement to say, "The Lamanites are *among* the ancestors of the American Indians." One has to wonder if the church changed the wording because of its awareness of the DNA evidence.

Beyond the Book of Mormon's DNA problem, it also has a problem when it comes to archaeology. Archaeology is the study of what has been left behind by earlier civilizations. Civilizations leave behind evidence of their existence.

In 1972 in *Dialogue* magazine, Michael Coe, a Yale University archaeologist, said, "The bare facts of the matter are that nothing, absolutely nothing, has ever shown up in any New World excavation which would suggest to a dispassionate observer that the Book of Mormon, as claimed by Joseph Smith, is a historical document relating to the history of early migrants to our hemisphere."

He was asked again in 1993 whether anything had changed, and his answer was that nothing had changed.

Closer to home, Dee Greene, an LDS archaeologist, said this about Book of Mormon archaeology: "The first myth we need to eliminate is that Book of Mormon archaeology exists. In order to have archaeology, you have to have data. We have no data. We know where Jerusalem and Jericho are. We do not know where Zarahemla or Bountiful or any other location from the Book of Mormon were or are."

The Book of Mormon cannot be placed in any real geographic location. Clearly, Joseph Smith believed that it took place in the eastern part of what is today the United States. After years of looking for archaeological evidence of cities from the Book of Mormon and finding no evidence, attention was turned to Central America as the possible scenario for the Book of Mormon. Once again, archaeologists have not found anything there that in any way relates to the Book of Mormon.

There are prominent Mormon intellectuals who have admitted the problems surrounding the historicity of the Book of Mormon. Prominent LDS historian Richard Bushman of Columbia University said in 2016 that "I think that for the Church to remain strong it has to reconstruct its narrative. The dominant narrative is not true; it can't be sustained. The Church has to absorb all this new information, or it will be on very shaky grounds and that's what it is trying to do, and it will be a strain for a lot of people, older people especially. But I think it has to change." Since he made that statement, Bushman has backtracked and said he still believes "in angels, plates, translations, and revelations."

The question is "why and how can he believe in those things?" How do Latter-day Saints "reconstruct the narrative"? How is it that people can be asked to believe in the Book of Mormon in spite of the lack of evidence?

The answer has to involve the way that Mormons see spiritual truth. Mormons believe that spiritual truth is known in a different way from all other truth.

Chapter 29
"How We Know"

Years ago, I was invited to attend a class at the Orem High School seminary. Seminaries sit adjacent to every high school in the state. Students are released one hour per day (on a voluntary basis) for classes that teach the basics of the LDS faith.

The class that I attended began with a lesson from the Book of Mormon. It began when the teacher pulled down a map of the Book of Mormon lands. He began by saying, "We do not know where any of this is, but let's just say Central America."

I wrote down in my notes that he had just admitted that the Book of Mormon could not be placed in any real-world context. He then went on and finished his lesson.

He ended the class by giving his testimony. He said that he believed that the Lord had used Joseph Smith and the Book of Mormon to restore the one true church in these latter days.

He then went beyond that and, in a tearful way, added these words: "I know that the Church is true when I look into the eyes of my son."

It struck me that in his experience of deep love for his child, this seminary teacher found evidence that the Book of Mormon and the LDS church were true.

He finished, and I looked around to see how the students in the class would respond. I had been a high school teacher in California. I expected to see some rolling of the eyes, maybe even some embarrassment or suppressed laughs, because in some ways, the teacher's presentation was over the top. There was none of that.

I looked around and there were tears in the eyes of some of these kids, and maybe even pride that their teacher had so boldly shared his testimony in the presence of the pastor from the church across the street.

As we left, a friend who had come with me said, "They have a completely different way of knowing what they know than we do."

How do they know what they know? How does one come to believe that the Book of Mormon is true? Mormons believe that spiritual truth is different from all other truth. It is determined by experience and faith.

Again, we look at the challenge given to every investigator into the church about the Book of Mormon. Moroni 10:4-5: "And when ye shall receive these things I would exhort you that ye would ask God the eternal father in the name of Christ, if these things are not true; and if ye shall ask with a sincere heart, with real intent, having faith in Christ, he will manifest the truth of it unto you by the power of the Holy Ghost. And by the power of the Holy Ghost ye may know the truth of all things."

Many have read those words and said, "What could be wrong with accepting this challenge?" After all, as you read the Book of Mormon it does sound a lot like the Bible, especially if you are familiar with the King James Version. What could be wrong with having more scripture and more truth?

The problem with Moroni 10:4 is that it leaves you with one of two choices. It says if you "pray with real intent having faith then you *will* receive a testimony that what you have just read is true." The result of this challenge is one of two things. You can either be an insincere non-Mormon or a sincere Mormon.

Not every testimony is the same, but usually it is some kind of positive, subjective experience. It used to be called a "burning in the bosom." Whatever that experience is, missionaries will tell the investigator that this is the Holy Spirit telling them that what they have read is true.

So powerful is the LDS testimony that it defies any evidence that you can throw against it. I had a friend in ministry here in Utah who asked a Mormon friend once, "If I could absolutely prove to you that the Book of Mormon was not true, would you stop believing in the LDS Church?"

He said, "no" because his testimony was that strong.

For a lot of Latter-day Saints, the power of their testimony lies *in the absence* of any objective evidence for the Book of Mormon. The absence of evidence means that you have to have greater faith. As it relates to the Book of Mormon, what Mormons are saying is that our subjective experiences are evidence that things happened the way the Book of Mormon says they happened.

I usually respond to this idea by talking about a personal experience I've had. It has to do with the movie *Field of Dreams*. Kevin Costner plays the role of Ray Kinsella in the movie. At the beginning of the movie, he hears a voice that says, "If you build it, he will come." Ray is a farmer in Iowa. He heeds the voice and builds a ball field out in the middle of his cornfield. He manicures it, puts lights on, and spends all of his savings on it.

Then one day, all of these long-dead, old-time, 1920s ball players come out of the cornfield and start playing baseball on his field. At the end of the movie, Ray's dad comes out of the cornfields as a young man. While his dad was alive, Ray and his dad were estranged from one another. There is this moment where Ray looks at his dad and says, "Hey, Dad, you want to have a catch?"

I saw that movie for the first time with my dad. My dad and I had spent a lot of time playing catch when I was young. As we watched that movie together, we both fell apart. I had a deep and profoundly moving experience. So did my Dad. We were both crying like babies.

Several years later, I watched *Field of Dreams* with my son Robbie, who was 13 at the time. As we watched the ending of the movie, once again I was in tears. That movie expresses a truth that runs incredibly deep . . . that has to do with the relationships between fathers and sons. It was an overwhelming, overpowering spiritual experience.

Here is the question. "Because I had that experience watching *Field of*

Dreams, does that mean that dead men have walked out of cornfields and played baseball in Iowa?" No, it doesn't.

The reality is that there is more evidence for the movie *Field of Dreams* than there is for the Book of Mormon because at least we know there's an Iowa. I have even been to the place in Iowa where the movie was filmed.

Feelings and emotions play a role in our faith. Truth can and often does create emotions, but emotions do not create objective reality.

No matter how strongly one might feel about the Book of Mormon, powerful feelings cannot make the events and places that are recorded in the book real. When it comes to the places, people, and events in the book, we need some corroborating evidence for the central events of the Book of Mormon. There are none.

The main reason I am not a Mormon is that I do not believe the Book of Mormon is true. If the Book of Mormon is not true, then Joseph Smith cannot be a prophet because Joseph Smith based his entire prophetic mission on the foundation of that book. If Joseph Smith is not a prophet, then the Church of Jesus Christ of Latter-day Saints is not the restoration of the one true church.

Many Latter-day Saints are coming to that conclusion. Our role as a church is not to argue people out of Mormonism. The Internet is filled with information about problematic issues related to the Book of Mormon and other truth claims of the LDS Church. In fact, some of the most effective writing has been produced by people who were or still are Latter-day Saints themselves.

One example is the CES letter (Church Education System) written in 2013 by Jeremy Runnels. In it, he asked questions regarding his concerns and doubts about the truth claims of the LDS Church. Many Mormons have read the letter written by Runnels. The end result was that three years later (as reported by the *Salt Lake Tribune* on April 24, 2016), Runnels resigned from the LDS Church.

Runnells stated that his church leaders had failed to answer his questions. He said, "It has become very clear to me that the church does not have answers to its truth crisis."

The evidence is overwhelming. Lots of Mormons have read this letter, or something like it, and come to the conclusion that the LDS Church is not what it claims to be. If the church is not true, then the question for any Latter-day Saint is "then what am I left with?"

This is a painful question. So many have invested so much in their faith. Our role as a local church is to help people answer that question. The fact that Mormonism is not true does not mean that Jesus isn't who he claimed to be, "the way the truth and the life." There is life and faith after Mormonism.

Chapter 30
Real Authority

As we go back to the conversation between Jesus and the Samaritan woman, we can see that this woman filters everything that Jesus has told her through her understanding of the conflict between Jews and Samaritans.

In Verse 21, she says, "Our ancestors worshiped on this mountain, but you Jews claim that the place where we must worship is in Jerusalem." She may be a failure as a Samaritan, but she does understand the conflict between Samaritans and Jews.

Jesus responds and says (John 4:21-24), "'Woman,' Jesus replied, 'Believe me, a time is coming when you will worship the Father neither on this mountain nor in Jerusalem. You Samaritans worship what you do not know; we worship what we do know, for salvation is from the Jews. Yet a time is coming and has now come when the true worshipers will worship the Father in Spirit and in truth, for they are the kind of worshipers the Father seeks. God is spirit, and his worshipers must worship in the Spirit and in truth.'"

Jesus is letting her in on the fact that something new is happening that is going to make the centuries-old conflict between Jews and Samaritans irrelevant. A time has come when it no longer matters what Jews and Samaritans are saying.

The only thing that matters is who is God and what is God saying to us?

Jesus does let this Samaritan woman know what he thinks of Samaritan claims to authority. He says, "You Samaritans worship what you do not know; we worship what we do know, for salvation is from the Jews." Jesus says, in effect, "You Samaritans are wrong, and Jews are right about something."

Any claim to authority that the Jews had comes from this simple fact: Salvation comes from the Jews. The reason that Jesus could say salvation is from the Jews is because Jesus is a Jew, and salvation comes from Him.

Mormonism claims to have authority to speak for God through a living prophet. Hebrews 1:1-2 is telling at this point. "In the past God spoke to our forefathers through the prophets at many times and in various ways. But in these last days He has spoken to us by his Son whom He appointed heir of all things and through whom He made the universe." This passage is telling us that we no longer need human beings to speak for us because God has spoken through His Son.

Jesus reveals God fully and finally. John 1:1: "In the beginning was the Word, and the Word was with God, and the Word was God." Just like our words express who we are, the Word of God (Jesus) expresses who God is. John 1:14: "The Word became flesh and made his dwelling among us." Jesus speaks for God. He is our authority.

Jesus makes that claim in Matthew 28:18: "All authority is given to me in Heaven and on Earth." When Jesus claimed all authority in Heaven and on Earth, the disciples believed Him. They believed Him because they had just experienced something.

The same Jesus who was speaking those words in Matthew 28 had shortly before this died on a cross and was now very much alive. Based on that reality, the disciples obeyed Jesus when he commanded them to "go and make disciples of all nations." We believe that Jesus has all authority in Heaven and on Earth because he has been raised from the dead.

We are living at a different time. Jesus has ascended into Heaven, and the disciples of Jesus have passed away. The question for us now is "who speaks for Jesus?" The simple answer to that question is the Bible.

The Bible consists of two parts. The first part is the Old Testament. These were the scriptures that existed when Jesus was on this earth. These were the scriptures Paul wrote of when he said in 1 Corinthians 15:3-4, "For what I received I passed on to you as of first importance: that Christ died for our sins according to the scriptures, that he was buried, that he was raised on the third day according to the scriptures."

I love the account of Jesus after the Resurrection where he meets two disciples on the road to Emmaus. Luke 24:27: "And beginning with Moses and all the prophets, he explained to them what was said in all the scriptures concerning himself." As Jesus walked along the road with these two disciples, He showed them how the Old Testament pointed to Him.

As Jesus walked with those two disciples on the road to Emmaus, the New Testament was yet to be written. Where did the New Testament come from?

The disciples who Jesus left behind now became known as "apostles" or "sent ones." Jesus told them in Acts 1:8, "You will be my witnesses in Jerusalem, and in all Judea and Samaria, and to the ends of the Earth." They were not only tasked with taking the good news to the nations; these apostles also were the primary witnesses to the truth about Jesus. They became the custodians of the faith.

From day one, the church recognized this. The church "devoted themselves to the apostles teaching" (Acts 2:42). The apostles teaching became the standard of truth for the church. The apostles went into the world and made disciples, and the church experienced explosive growth. As the disciples grew older, and as the persecution of the church became more intense, the apostles became concerned with how the faith would be passed on to the next generation.

The apostles began to put their testimony of Jesus in written form. The crucifixion and resurrection occurred around 30 AD. The writing of the New Testament probably begins around 50 AD. The New Testament is produced in the generation when the apostles were still alive, and it was produced through their ministry.

One of the advantages of ministry in Utah is that we are dealing with people who have some knowledge of the Bible. They know and love the stories of Jesus. There is a way in which people's experience in Mormonism can build a bridge that leads them to faith. Mormons also have some ideas about the Bible that make it difficult to trust the Bible.

The LDS Church does accept the Bible as scripture. It also accepts the Book of Mormon (along with the Pearl of Great Price and Doctrine & Covenants) as scripture. The whole idea behind the Book of Mormon is that the Bible itself is somehow incomplete. We see that in 2 Nephi 29:6, which says, "Thou fool, that shall say: a Bible, we have got a Bible, and we need no more Bible."

Not only that, but the eighth article of faith of the LDS Church states clearly that the Bible has been subject to corruption: "We believe the Bible to be the word of God as far as it is translated correctly; we also believe the Book of Mormon to be the word of God." This article of faith calls into question whether or not the text we have of the Bible reflects the words of the original authors.

When people from an LDS background come to CenterPoint and to other evangelical churches in Utah, they are introduced to a different way of looking at the Bible. We believe that the Bible can be trusted. We believe that when it comes to the actual text of the Bible. This is backed by scholarship. New Testament scholar F.F. Bruce stated that "the evidence for our New Testament writings is ever so much greater than the evidence for many writings of classical authors, the authenticity of which no one dreams of questioning. And if the New Testament were a collection of secular writings, their authenticity would generally be regarded as beyond all doubt." (F.F. Bruce, *The New Testament Documents: Are They Reliable?* 1981, p. 10)

This does not mean there are no questions related to the text of the Bible. Every ancient book has gone through a process of being copied by hand and then recopied. There are so many manuscripts, and there is so much agreement between those manuscripts, that the best estimates are that at most, half of one percent of the readings are in doubt.

Do those variants have any impact on the essentials of the Christian faith? New Testament scholar Craig Blomberg states, "Essential Christian beliefs are not affected by textual variants in the manuscript tradition of the New Testament." (Craig Blomberg, *Can We Still Believe the Bible?*)

One of the things you will hear from critics of the Christian faith is that the New Testament was written two or three centuries after the fact. If that is the case, then we do have a real problem. If the New Testament was written two and three centuries after the fact, the people who wrote it would have to have been liars because they claimed to be eyewitnesses.

William F Albright was the world's foremost biblical archaeologist. He stated, "We can already say emphatically that there is no longer any solid basis for dating any book of the NT after about 80 AD. That is 50 years after the death of Christ." All these books were written in the time when there were eyewitnesses who were still alive.

Who are you going to trust to tell you the truth about any event? Someone who lived through it, or someone who wrote hundreds of years later? We believe in the Resurrection for the same reason that we believe in any other event of history. We believe the witnesses to the event are reliable. They are writing about real places and real people.

One of the things Mormons will say when confronted with the lack of evidence for the Book of Mormon is that the Bible has the same problems. This is simply not true. Unlike the Book of Mormon, the Bible is set in a very real place in a very real time.

Phillip Jenkins, religion professor from Baylor University said, "You can't dig a hole in Jerusalem without finding something to indicate that something like the world portrayed in the Bible existed there thousands of years ago." (Anxious Bench blog, May 17, 2015.)

In March of 2020, my wife and I visited Israel and were amazed by how many places and ruins you can find from the time of the Bible. As you drive through Israel, the places talked about in the Bible—Jerusalem, Bethlehem, the Sea of Galilee, the River Jordan, and Nazareth—are all still there. The Bible is set in a very real place in a very real time period with people who really lived.

There are no places like that when it comes to the Book of Mormon. Phillip Jenkins asks the question, "Does the Book of Mormon contain a statement or idea about the New World that Joseph Smith could not have known at the time, but which has subsequently been validated by archaeological or historical research?" The answer is no.

I once was at a luncheon at BYU where pastors from Utah were invited. I found myself sitting next to Bill Heersink, a fellow pastor in Utah. Next to him was BYU professor Truman Madsen, who was the founder and director of BYU's Jerusalem Center.

Dr. Madsen was Harvard-educated and a leading LDS intellectual. Pastor Heersink asked Dr. Madsen if it created tension for BYU students at the Jerusalem Center to be in a place where biblical archaeology was alive and well, and then not have a similar place in the New World where the events of the Book of Mormon played out? He admitted that it was a problem, and we moved onto another subject.

We believe the 27 books of the New Testament were written about a time and place which really existed. The Bible is not just a book written about real events in real places, it was written by real people. The Bible is true to life. The Bible is not written as legend, where there are heroes and villains. The main figures in the Bible are real people.

The Book of Mormon provides us with a contrast. In the Book of Mormon, so often the characters are seen as either good people or bad people. In the Bible, we see the heroes of the faith demonstrating great faith. Along with that, we also see that they can look weak, selfish, clueless, and petty.

Part of the power of the Bible is that we can relate to the people in the Bible. It is written about people like us. Rather than dismissing the Bible because of all of the bad examples of human behavior, the Bible gives us hope. It shows us how God works in people's lives with the same kinds of failings we have.

We can trust the Bible. We can trust the authenticity of the biblical text. It was written about real people in real places and times. That is not where I want to stop with my Mormon friends.

There is a deeper question I want to answer. It is not, "How come you are not a Mormon?"

The real question is, "Why am I a Christian?"

Surprisingly, the answer is not simply because I believe the Bible.

Chapter 31
The Reason We Believe

A lot of critics of the Christian faith will say something like this about the truth claims of Christianity: "You seek to prove what you believe about Jesus by going to the Bible. I don't believe in the Bible. Case closed."

This is where the Christian faith is unique. The Christian faith was not created by a book. It was created by an event. That event is the Resurrection. The Resurrection created a movement, and that movement created the New Testament.

In contrast, in the LDS Church, the great foundational miracle of Mormonism was that an angel directed Joseph Smith to golden plates that were translated by Joseph Smith, and that translation became the Book of Mormon. The book created the movement. In a similar manner, Islam was created by a book. Muslims claim that the Koran was given to Mohammed by God. The Koran created Islam.

Before the New Testament was written, there was a "Jesus movement." There was a thriving Jesus movement in the first century of Jesus followers throughout the Roman Empire. The greatest evidence of what that movement was like is found in the New Testament.

We see proof of that movement outside of the Bible. Suetonius was a Roman historian who was the author of *The Lives of the Twelve Caesars*. He wrote that during the reign of the Emperor Claudius (41-54 AD), the Jews had been expelled from Rome at the "instigation of Chrestus." Historians believe that the Jewish community in Rome was divided over Christ and that the division was large enough that Claudius took notice and had all Jews expelled from Rome. Clearly there was a growing Jesus movement in the first century Roman Empire.

Something created the Jesus movement. What was it that motivated the earliest followers of Jesus? The Apostle Paul makes it clear that it was the resurrection of Jesus. 1 Corinthians 15:14-15: "If Christ has not been raised, our preaching is useless and so is your faith. More than that, we are then found to be false witnesses about God, for we have testified about God that he raised Christ from the dead."

So much was at stake in the apostle's conviction that Jesus was alive that Paul goes on and says that if this is not true, if Christ has not been raised from the dead, they (the apostles) "are to be pitied above all men" (1 Corinthians 15:19). Paul also recognizes that if Christ is risen, then Jesus is who He claimed to be. As Paul says in Romans 1:4, Jesus "was declared the Son of God with power by the resurrection from the dead."

The Jesus movement was created by an event—the Resurrection. Why do we believe in the Resurrection? The most compelling reasons have to do with the witnesses to the resurrection. In 1 Corinthians 15:5-8, Paul seeks to give the evidence for the resurrection by listing some of the appearances of Jesus.

Paul says, "He appeared to Cephas, and then to the Twelve. After that, He appeared to more than five hundred of the brothers and sisters at the same time, most of whom are still living, though some have fallen asleep. Then He appeared to James, then to all the apostles, and last of all He appeared to me also, as to one abnormally born."

The witnesses to the Resurrection did not believe that Jesus had been raised from the dead because they had some sort of emotional, subjective spiritual experience. They believed because they encountered the risen Christ. They were eyewitnesses.

1 John 1:1: "That which was from the beginning, which we have heard, which we have seen with our eyes, which we have looked at and our hands

have touched—this we proclaim concerning the Word of life." John, speaking for the apostles, says in effect, "I was there. I heard Him. I saw Him. I touched Him."

We not only have witnesses to the resurrection, but I find that they are the kind of witnesses that are believable. As you look at the apostles' testimony of the events surrounding the crucifixion and resurrection, you try and discern their motivation for telling their story. It could not have been to make themselves look good.

At the Last Supper, we have the disciples arguing about who will be the greatest in the Kingdom of Heaven. We are told in Mark 14:50, "Meanwhile (after Jesus was arrested) all of his disciples deserted him and ran away."

During the trial of Jesus, Peter is asked on three different occasions if he is one of the disciples of Jesus. This is the same Peter who has just said that even if everyone else fell away, he would be willing to die with Jesus. Each time, Peter denies Jesus.

On Sunday morning, where do we find the disciples? They are hiding behind closed doors. They cannot summon the courage to accompany the women who wanted to go to the tomb so they could properly take care of the body of Jesus. That is when Jesus makes his first appearance to Mary Magdalene and some of the others. Those women then run and tell the disciples that the tomb is empty.

This means that the first witnesses to the resurrection of Jesus are women. If you were making a story up in the first century and you wanted to get people to believe you, you would not make women the first witnesses to the resurrection. Women were not trusted in that day to give testimony in court because they were seen as unreliable.

One of the earliest critics of the Christian faith was a man named Celsus, who wrote at the end of the 2nd century. One of his main arguments against the resurrection was that the earliest witnesses were women and that women could not be trusted.

Why would the gospel writers portray women as the first witnesses? Could it be that this was the way things happened, and that the writers of the gospels are committed to telling the truth about what happened?

After hearing what these women have said, Peter and John run to the tomb and they find the tomb empty. Then Jesus starts showing up in many different places to many different people.

The thing we cannot help but notice about the disciples is that their experience of the risen Christ changes them. They are so certain Jesus is alive that they go from being cowards hiding behind closed doors to men willing to go out and spread the message that Jesus had come out of the grave alive. They believed it so strongly that they were willing to die for it. What would possibly convince them to do that? They could not deny what they had seen.

What we hear at this point is that "a lot of people have died for what they believe." People have died for their faith in a book. People have died for their faith in the Book of Mormon. Many more have died for their faith in the Koran. The writing of a book does not require a miracle. Bringing to life someone who is dead *does* require a miracle.

I am a Christian because I believe in the resurrection. I believe in the resurrection because I believe the testimony of the apostles. Their witness and testimony don't need to be added to. In fact, it cannot be added to because it is an eyewitness, firsthand testimony. This is why we do not need additional scripture beyond what the apostles have given us.

One question that is often asked is, "What about all of the other gospels that are not included in the New Testament? There are other gospels written, like the Gospel of Thomas. Why aren't they included in the New Testament?"

The reason is simply that they were not apostolic. They were not produced through the ministry of the apostles. They were not written during the generation when the eyewitnesses were still alive.

The Gospel of Thomas was written well over a century after the death and resurrection of Jesus. That would be like me claiming to write a firsthand account of the Civil War. You would know that my book was not authentic because I was not alive during the Civil War. I could write about what it was like to grow up in the 1960s. I could not write something firsthand about the 1860s.

Whenever you have something that is original and has great value, people want to counterfeit it. Many have tried to bring us a counterfeit Jesus. Jesus promised that this would happen. Matthew 24:11: ". . . and many false prophets will appear and deceive many people."

We can see through the history of the Church that when people attempted to create new scripture, it was to present to us a different Jesus. Mormonism gives us a different Jesus.

The LDS Church is not alone. I have spoken on occasion outside of Utah and have begun a number of talks this way: "I want to tell you about an uneducated young man who claimed to have received a visitation from an angel. He claims that an angel told him that all of the other religions were false and that he was going to restore the one true faith to the earth. To confirm this, he was given a new book of scripture that was proof of his prophetic status. This young man was persecuted for his beliefs but against all odds, this new faith survived and is growing rapidly all over the world."

When I ask, "Who am I talking about?" people will say Joseph Smith because they know I am from Utah. The same things also apply to Mohammed. Mohammed and Joseph Smith both had humble beginnings. Both founded new religions when an angel appeared to them and revealed to them new scriptures. Both religions claim these scriptures are miracles since their authors were the most simple and uneducated of men.

Mohammed and Joseph Smith both said that Jews and Christians had corrupted their scriptures and religion. Islam also has a place for Jesus in its theology. He is not the Son of God but the second-greatest prophet after Mohammed.

Who are we going to believe about Jesus? Mohammed and Joseph Smith say, "Believe me because I have this book and an angel gave it to me." We can believe them, or we can trust those eyewitnesses that gave us the New Testament.

The Bible has been attacked for 20 centuries, but it has stood the test of time. The reason it has stood the test of time is because of its message.

The Bible is an amazing collection of 66 books written by 40 different authors over a 1500-year period with a common theme. The message of the Bible is the salvation of the world through Jesus Christ. That speaks to the inspiration of the Bible. How do you find 40 people to agree on anything?

The answer is that even though there were 40 authors, there was really one author behind it. God inspired the different Bible writers to communicate the truth about Jesus in their own style through their own unique set of circumstances. Altogether, the Bible provides us with an incredibly compelling picture of Jesus. As the Bible points us to Jesus, he answers our deepest human needs. He answers the needs of the people that we minister to here in Utah Valley.

- People are lost. Jesus said, "For the Son of Man came to seek and to save what was lost." (Luke 19:10)
- People are living with shame, guilt, and regret. "Jesus is the lamb of God that takes away the sin of the world." (John 1:29)
- People are empty. Jesus said, "I have come that they might have life and have it to the full." (John 10:10)
- People are looking for truth. Jesus says, "I am the way, the truth, the life." (John 14:6)
- You see people looking for someone to trust, and Jesus says, "I am the good shepherd." (John 10:11)
- You see people looking for someone to worship. Jesus said, "Before Abraham was, I AM." (John 8:58)

Jesus uses this book to change lives. We have seen that among Latter-day Saints. When I ask former Mormons the question, "What is it that changed for you?" part of the answer is that they started to read the Bible and look at it in a brand-new way. They see that the Bible is really about Jesus. They do not start worshiping the Bible, but they begin to worship Jesus, the one that the Bible reveals.

Chapter 32
The One True Church

If we look back at John 4:21, the Samaritan woman asked Jesus where the one true place of worship was to be found. "You Jews say Jerusalem, our Samaritan fathers say that it is on this mountain." She thought that the great quest of life was to find the one true religion. In our context, Latter-day Saints believe that the great spiritual search of life is to find the one true church. They see themselves as that church.

They believe that they have special places (temples) where special people (a priesthood) can perform special rituals that bring people into relationship with God. Was the mission of Jesus to come to Earth and organize the one true church and give it the authority to save and exalt?

No one is a bigger proponent of the role of the local church than I am. The local church plays a vital role in what God is doing on Earth. The ultimate reason that Jesus came to Earth was not to create an organization. God is doing something greater.

John 4:23: "Yet a time is coming and has now come when the true worshipers will worship the Father in the Spirit and in truth, for they are the kind of worshipers the Father seeks."

God is looking for worshipers. From the beginning, God has always wanted to be with His people. The right response to the presence of God in our lives is worship. In the Old Testament, God was with His people in the Tabernacle. God lived in a special place: a room called the Holy of Holies in the Tabernacle. Later on, the Temple was built. In that Temple, there was once again the Holy of Holies.

When Jesus arrived on Earth, God became present on Earth in a brand-new way. God was present in the body of Jesus. In John 2:21, Jesus goes so far as to call his body "the temple." After Jesus is raised from the dead and ascends into Heaven, He sends the Holy Spirit to live in those that belong to him. We become the temple.

He lives in us as individual believers. "Don't you know that your bodies are the temple of the Holy Spirit?" (1 Corinthians 6:19) He also lives in this thing called the church, the body of Christ. "Don't you know that you yourselves are God's temple and that God's Spirit dwells in your midst?" (Corinthians 3:16)

God lives in us individually and corporately. The church is the body of Christ. Today, the church is the primary means by which God is present in the world. God is doing something through the church in the world. What is God doing? Jesus answers that question in Matthew 16. This is one of only two times that Jesus speaks of the church.

On this occasion, Jesus is alone with his disciples and asks them, "Who do people say that I am?" They give various answers, and then Peter steps forward and says, "You are the Christ, the Son of the Living God."

Jesus responds and tells Peter and the rest of the disciples, "And I tell you that you are Peter, and on this rock I will build my church, and the gates of Hades will not overcome it. I will give you the keys of the Kingdom of Heaven; whatever you bind on Earth will be bound in Heaven, and whatever you loose on Earth will be loosed in Heaven." (Matthew 16:18-19)

This is the definitive passage on the church in the New Testament. Mormons have a take on this passage. Latter-day Saints claim that they are the church that Jesus is referring to in Matthew 16. Latter-day Saints believe that the church Jesus founded went into apostasy and ceased to exist around the end of the first century. The one true church did not exist until it was restored by God through Joseph Smith in 1830.

One problem with that view is that in Verse 18, Jesus says of the church that "the gates of Hades will not prevail against it." If there was a universal apostasy and restoration, then the church was prevailed against and Jesus was wrong. The truth is that nothing can or ever will prevail against the church.

The church that Jesus is speaking of here is the one true church. This is the Universal Church, which consists of all those that belong to Jesus Christ by faith, wherever they are found.

If there has been a universal apostasy, then Jesus failed to keep the promise he made in Matthew 28 where he tells the apostles to go and make disciples of all nations and he promises that "surely I am with you always, to the very end of the age."

No one has stated this more beautifully than Bishop J.C. Ryle. He said of the church, "Nothing can altogether overthrow and destroy it. Its members may be persecuted, oppressed, imprisoned, beaten, beheaded, burned; but the true church is never altogether extinguished; it rises again from its afflictions; it lives on through fire and water. When crushed in one land it springs up in another."

Then, speaking of the different attempts to destroy the church through the ages, Ryle said, "The church is an anvil that has broken many a hammer in this world."

In Greek, the word for church is "ekklesia." It does not refer to a building, or an organization. It refers to a people. It literally means "called-out ones." It refers to any gathering of His people.

Jesus refers to the church as "my church." It is his because He bought it. The price He paid was his blood (Acts 20:28). The church is a people called out by God into a relationship with Himself through Jesus.

When you build, you begin with a foundation. Jesus looks at Peter and says, ". . . you are Peter (the Greek word for rock), and on this rock I will build my church."

What was Jesus saying to Peter? Was Jesus saying, "Peter, you are the man. You are so rock-solid that I am going to build my Church, my eternal purposes, on you"? I don't think that was what Jesus meant.

In just a few moments, Jesus is going to tell the disciples that he is going to be rejected and that he is going to be killed. Peter hears this and takes Jesus aside and begins to scold Him.

Jesus then says to Peter, "Get behind me, Satan." Later on, when Jesus is arrested and tried, Peter denies knowing Jesus three times. Peter is no rock.

It is important to note that when Jesus says, "You are Peter" he uses the word "petros" (little rock) and then says, "on this Petra" (big rock) "I will build my church."

What is the big rock? Peter has just made his confession that "Jesus is the Christ, the Son of the Living God." The big rock that Jesus is talking about is not one man, or a group of men. The rock is Peter's confession that Jesus is the Christ, the Son of the Living God.

The foundation, the rock upon which the church is built, is the truth about who Jesus is. Our foundation is Jesus. How do we know about Jesus? The church is built on the foundation of the apostles' testimony about Jesus. We know about Jesus from Peter and the rest of the apostles. That is why Paul writes in Ephesians 2:20 that "the church is built on the foundation of the apostles and the prophets but that Christ himself is the chief cornerstone."

From its beginning, the church has been devoted to "the apostles' teaching" (Acts 2:42). The church in Jerusalem could devote themselves to the apostles' teaching because the apostles were right there with them, teaching them.

Today, we find the apostles teaching in the New Testament. What the whole New Testament has in common is that it comes from the ministry of the apostles.

This is something that the church was committed to on its first day, and it is something that it will be committed to on the last day.

The New Testament does not just talk about the Universal Church, it talks about the local church. Local churches are visible representatives of Jesus in the places in which they are located. The local church is where believers gather together to fulfill the commands of Christ. The Universal

Church is permanent; the local church is not. Lots can change about the local church.

When it comes to the actual form the church takes, there is actually very little that cannot change. The music we worship with, the clothes people wear, the order of service, the day and time of worship, the name a church goes by, where the church meets, and even how the church is organized, can all change. Local churches can even cease to exist.

How is the local church a part of the Universal Church? What makes us a part of that great building? There are two ways where the local church participates in building the Universal Church. The first way is that the local church is called to build on the rock Jesus spoke of in Matthew 16. The church builds on the foundation that is the truth about Jesus.

A church must continue to build on the rock, or it ceases to be the church. 1 Corinthians 3:11: "No one can lay any other foundation than the one we already have—Christ Jesus." The church cannot change foundations. We must continue to build on the rock which is Jesus. That rock that Jesus spoke of is the apostles' teachings, which are found in the Bible.

There is another way in which the local church builds the Universal Church. We participate in the purpose that Jesus has for his church. That purpose is found in what Jesus says next in Matthew 16:19: "I will give you the keys of the Kingdom of Heaven; whatever you bind on Earth will be bound in Heaven, and whatever you loose on Earth will be loosed in Heaven."

Jesus has given the church something to do in this world. He has given the church keys to use that open the door to the Kingdom of Heaven. When the church stops using the keys that Jesus has given it to open those doors, it ceases to be what Jesus created it to be. What are those keys?

Latter-day Saints have an answer to that question. They believe that when Jesus gave Peter the keys to the Kingdom of Heaven, he and the rest of the apostles were given authority. The apostles then ordained others, who yet ordained others. But somewhere at the end of the first century, that authority was lost.

They believe that apostolic authority did not return to Earth again until Peter, James, and John showed up on the banks of the Susquehanna River and ordained Joseph Smith to the Melchizedek priesthood. The LDS Church believes that Joseph Smith in time ordained others, and from that succession of ordination, the LDS Church believes that today there are men on Earth who have the priesthood and possess the keys of the Kingdom of Heaven.

D & C 84:21: "And without the ordinances thereof, and the authority of the priesthood, the power of godliness is not manifest unto men in the flesh." Mormons believe they have possession of this priesthood and, by virtue of the power they have received, the authority to perform ceremonies like baptism that allow people to enter into the Kingdom of Heaven.

Do rituals save? Some verses in the Bible would seem to indicate that baptism is necessary for salvation. One would be Acts 2:38, which says, "Repent and be baptized, every one of you, in the name of Jesus Christ for the forgiveness of your sins." There are a whole host of other salvation verses, like Ephesians 2:8-9, Romans 10:9, and Titus 3:5, that say nothing of baptism in relationship to salvation.

1 Corinthians 1 is a telling passage of scripture when it comes to Paul's attitude about baptism. He was addressing the division going on in the Corinthian Church over people dividing up based on which human leader they followed. Paul says in verses 12-13, "One of you says, 'I follow Paul'; another, 'I follow Apollos'; another, 'I follow Cephas'; still another, 'I follow Christ.' Is Christ divided?"

People were actually claiming a certain amount of status based on who they were baptized by. Paul corrects them by saying in 1:13-16, "Were you baptized in the name of Paul? I thank God that I did not baptize any of you except Crispus and Gaius, so no one can say that you were baptized in my name. (Yes, I also baptized the household of Stephanas; beyond that, I don't remember if I baptized anyone else.)"

What is relevant for us is that the LDS Church tells us it makes all the difference in the world who we are baptized by. If you are not baptized by someone with priesthood authority, you are just taking a bath. In this passage, Paul does not remember beyond a few people who he baptized. If baptism is required for salvation, Paul should have worked at remembering or at least kept better records about who he did or did not baptize.

The most relevant thing for us is found in Verse 17: "For Christ did not send me to baptize, but to preach the gospel." This verse is a problem for anyone who believes that the LDS Church is the restoration of the one true church and has been given the authority to perform ordinances that save and exalt. If that is true, then how could Paul say that Christ didn't send him to baptize, but to preach the gospel? If the LDS Church is what it claims to be, then baptism by one having priesthood authority *is* the gospel.

The gospel, however, is that we are saved through faith alone in Christ alone, and the importance of baptism is that it is a symbol of that. Baptism is an outward demonstration of the inward reality that I am in Christ. Baptism is a symbol that my sins have died in Christ, and that I have new life in Him.

I do not need a human priesthood in order to gain entrance into the presence of God. We have Jesus, who is our great high priest. 1 Timothy 2:5: "For there is one God and one mediator between God and mankind, the man Christ Jesus." We now have direct access to God through Jesus.

The reality is that he has made us priests. Peter speaks to the church in 1 Peter 2:9 and says, "But you are a chosen people, a royal priesthood, a holy nation, a people belonging to God, that you may declare the praises of Him who called you out of darkness into his wonderful light."

To be a priest is to have access to God and to be able to go to God on behalf of others. If you have received Jesus Christ and believe in Him, then He has made you his child. If there is one thing that is true of children, it is that they have access to their parents. We belong to God's family and have direct access to Him. It does not matter if you are male, female, Jew, Greek, slave, free, millionaire, or homeless—if you belong to Jesus Christ by faith, then you are family. We have the right to come into His presence.

When Jesus tells Peter and the apostles that he is giving them the keys of the Kingdom of Heaven, he is giving them not only access but authority to act on his behalf. The keys themselves do something—they open the door to the Kingdom of Heaven.

What opens the door to the Kingdom of Heaven? It would make sense that it has something to do with what Peter has just said, "You are the Christ, the Son of the Living God." Peter has just told the truth about Jesus. In time, Jesus is going to send Peter and the rest of the apostles into the world with the message that "Jesus is the Christ, the Son of the Living God."

The keys are the gospel. The gospel message opens the door to the Kingdom of Heaven. Do we have the keys? Yes, we do. The gospel is preached today as it has been in every generation. That message still changes lives and opens the doors to the Kingdom of Heaven. That message has power: "Whatever you bind on Earth will be bound in Heaven, and whatever you loose on Earth will be loosed in Heaven."

The natural way to take those words is that they refer to the two things that a key will do. A key either opens a door (looses it) or it locks a door (binds it). The New Living Translation gets it right here when it says, "Whatever you lock on Earth will be locked in Heaven. Whatever you open on Earth will be opened in Heaven."

By preaching the good news, people will have an opportunity to respond. If they say yes, the door is opened. If they say no, the door remains closed. What Jesus is saying to Peter is that the decisions people make here on Earth about the message you are going to preach are going to impact eternity.

There is something else important about a key. Not any key will do. If I lock my car keys into my Mazda and I come to you and you have a Ford and I say, "Can I borrow your keys so I can open the door to my car?" you would tell me that your keys will not help me. For a key to work, it has to be the right shape. It has to have the right code.

What is the key that opens the door to the Kingdom of Heaven? If you look at the apostles' message, it is not that any key will do. There is a message that opens the door, and no other message will save. That message is not "do your best to try and be a good person." It is not "follow the rules and then we will see how you compare to everyone else." It is not that the key is finding someone with the authority to baptize us.

Our greatest need is for someone to do something about our sin. Sin has a consequence. Because of it, we experience death. We are dead spiritually, and we are dying physically. On the cross, Jesus took the death that our sins deserve. When He was raised from the dead, He defeated sin and death. If we receive Him, we don't have to experience eternal separation from God. We can live eternally with Him. That is the good news. That is the key that opens the door of the Kingdom of Heaven. No other key will do.

Jesus has given us those keys. When Jesus gave the keys to Peter, He was doing more than giving Peter the truth about who He is. When you give your keys to someone, you are saying something about your relationship with them. My life is on my key ring. If I give you my keys (and in this computer age, if I give you my passwords) I will be giving you access to my life.

There is a group of people I have given my keys to. Those people are my family. They have access to the house, to my cars, to my office. They have access to my life.

Who does Jesus give His keys to? He gives them to His family. John 1:12-13: "But to all who did receive Him, who believed in His name, He gave the right to become children of God, who were born, not of blood nor of the will of the flesh nor of the will of man, but of God."

Jesus does more than give us a job to do. He has made us His children. He wants us to be involved in what He is doing. He wants us in the family business. We need to realize that, as believers, Jesus has given us this incredible authority to represent Him and bring people into His presence.

Chapter 33
The God We Worship

What do we do in the presence of God? When we come into the presence of God, we worship. John 4:23: "Yet a time is coming and has now come when the true worshipers will worship the Father in the Spirit and in truth, for they are the kind of worshipers the Father seeks." The Father is looking for worshipers. He is not looking for just any kind of worshiper. He is looking for worshipers that will worship him in spirit and in truth. To worship God in truth is to worship the God who is. The God who is, is the only God worthy of our worship.

We were created to worship. It is important to see that when God gives Moses the Ten Commandments, the first two have to do with worship. Exodus 20:3-5: "You shall have no other gods before me." Then God says, "You shall not make for yourself an image in the form of anything in heaven above or on the earth beneath or in the waters below. You shall not bow down to them or worship them." God gave his people those commandments because it is in our fallen nature to worship things not worthy of our worship. In the time when these commands were given, people worshiped all sorts of gods. Those gods were either creatures or something that people created.

It is our nature to worship. G.K. Chesterton once said, "When men choose not to believe in God, they do not thereafter believe in nothing, they then become capable of believing in anything." In our day, that "anything" can include money, fame, power, celebrity, or pleasure. Our pursuit of something worthy of our worship only leads to frustration because only the LORD is truly worthy of our worship.

The Apostle Paul lived in a culture similar to ours with all sorts of options when it came to worship. 1 Corinthians 8:5-6: "For even if there are so-called gods, whether in Heaven or on Earth (as indeed there are many 'gods' and many 'lords'), yet for us there is but one God, the Father, from whom all things came and for whom we live; and there is but one Lord, Jesus Christ, through whom all things came and through whom we live."

Paul is saying that even though there are all sorts of gods out there, there is only one God that is worthy of our worship. It matters what we believe about God. A.W. Tozer once said, "What comes into **our** minds when we think about God is **the** most important thing about us."

In John 4:24, Jesus tells this Samaritan woman something about God that is essential to knowing who God is. He says that "God is spirit." He does not say that God is spiritual or that God has a spirit. He says that God *is* Spirit. That is God's nature.

This means that God does not exist the way that anything else in the universe exists. We do not exist the way that God exists. We are physical beings living in space and time. The truth that the Bible reveals about God is that God created and spoke this space, time, and matter universe into existence. He is before it. Everything within the universe was caused. But no one caused God to come into existence.

The very name of God in the Old Testament, "Yahweh," is an expression of this. The Name means "I Am that I Am." It tells us that God is the source of all existence. He is the one whose existence does not depend on anyone or anything else. God has always been God. Psalm 90:2: "From everlasting to everlasting, you are God."

The God of the Bible is different from the God of Mormonism. Shortly before he died in 1844, Joseph Smith claimed to reveal the truth about God that had been hidden and lost since the time of the early church. He said, "God himself was once as we are now, and is an exalted man, and sits enthroned in yonder heavens! . . . Here, then, is eternal life—to know the only wise and true God; and you have got to learn to be Gods yourselves, and to be kings and priests to God, the same as all Gods have done before you . . ."

Lorenzo Snow, the fifth president of the LDS Church, was being consistent with what Joseph Smith had said when he put the LDS view of God this way: "As man is, God once was, and as God is, man may become."

There has been a lot interaction between Mormons and evangelicals when it comes to the LDS view of God and that of biblical Christianity. There is a great deal of sensitivity among Mormon intellectuals when it comes to this discussion. This view of God makes Mormons different from traditional Christians. There are some that would want to distance themselves from the above statement by Lorenzo Snow.

Any time I've had conversations about these things, I have always tried to ask a clarifying question: "Has God always been God?" In the end, their answer has to be no.

BYU professor Robert Millet is a leading Mormon intellectual who has been involved in a number of dialogues with evangelicals over the last 20 years. Robert Millet says, "Latter-day Saints believe that God the Father is an exalted man, a corporeal being, a personage with flesh and bones . . . and that he grew and developed over time to become the Almighty that he now is. To say this another way, they [LDS] teach that God is all-powerful and all-knowing, but that he has not been so forever; there was once a time in an eternity past when he lived on an earth like ours." (*The Mormon Faith: A New Look at Christianity*, by Robert L. Millet, 1998, pp. 29-30)

The God of Mormonism is not fundamentally different from human beings in nature. Stephen Robinson, in the book *How Wide the Divide?* (page 18) says, "For LDS also believe in the literal fatherhood of God and brotherhood of humanity. We believe that God and human beings are the same species of being and that all men and women were his spiritual offspring in a pre-mortal existence."

In Christian theology, we speak of the communicable attributes of God. These are the characteristics of God that human beings can experience. Things like love, goodness, wisdom, justice, and truth. There are also the incommunicable attributes of God. These are things that God alone possesses and that we cannot experience. God is infinite, unchanging, all powerful, all knowing, present in all places. We cannot experience these things.

In one way, the incommunicable attributes of God do not exist for Mormons. The real difference between God and humans in Mormonism is not about the different natures of God and human beings. The difference is in the degree to which we as humans have progressed. All sorts of things follow from this view of God. If this is the case, then men are capable of becoming gods. If this is the case, then there are many gods in the universe.

This is a real problem for Mormons as they read the Bible. In Isaiah 43:10-12, God declares, "Before me no god was formed, nor will there be one after me. I, even I, am the Lord, and apart from me there is no savior." The God of the Bible has always been God. There was never a time when God was not God. The universe, on the other hand, has not always existed. We believe that God is infinite and that the material universe is finite. Mormons look at the world in a completely different way. They believe that the material universe has always existed, and God has not always been God.

Which view of the world fits best with modern scientific thought? I understand that many people of science reject the Bible. At the same time, modern scientific thought converges with the Bible in one important way: The universe had a beginning. What is called the Big Bang Theory has come to be the accepted explanation of the origin of how the universe came into existence. The universe is said to have come into existence in a singular moment where space, time, and matter began to exist.

In the ancient world, it was the commonly held belief that the material universe had always existed. There was this one exception. There was a tiny group of people, the Jews, that believed the universe had a beginning.

The Jewish scriptures, what Christians call the Old Testament, began with the words, "In the beginning God created the heavens and the earth."

Where modern science and the scriptures differ is that we claim to know The One who caused the world to come into existence. Jews and Christians (and we can include Muslims in this) understand that in order for the universe to exist there had to be someone/something to cause it to come into being. That being could not be part of the universe. That being would have to have existed before the universe. The Bible says that someone is God. Hebrews 11:3: "By faith we understand that the universe was formed at God's command, so that what is seen was not made out of what was visible."

The God of the Bible, who made all things out of nothing, is different from the God of Mormonism.

One of the things I have noticed about people when they leave the LDS Church is that when they do, they claim they no longer believe in God. Many will say that they have become "atheists." I understand why people leaving Mormonism would claim to no longer believe in God.

The reason for the "I am an atheist" statement from Mormons is that they have lived their lives with great certainty. They have believed that the church is true and that what the church teaches about God is true. When people leave the church, they are very hesitant to be certain of anything again. Saying that you are an atheist is a way of saying that "I do not know what I believe, and I do not want to be held to anything."

How do we respond when someone exiting Mormonism says they no longer believe in God? One response is to try and argue them into a belief in God. I would rather ask a question. My question to the former Mormon who now professes atheism is to ask them to "tell me about the God you no longer believe in."

When I have asked that question, sometimes people will look at me and wonder, "How can this guy be a pastor and not know who God is?" When they start telling me about the God they no longer believe in, at some point it becomes clear that they are talking about a God who is an exalted man.

At this point, I can say with complete sincerity, "If that is what it means to believe in God, then I guess that I am an atheist, because I do not believe in that God either."

It is interesting that in the early days of the Christian Church, Christians were called "atheist" because they did not believe in the kind of gods that everyone else in the Roman Empire believed in. People would ask, "Where is this God located? Where is his temple?"

I do not believe in a God that is located in space, time, and matter. I believe in a God who is one, who is spirit. I believe that God has made Himself known to us in the person of Jesus Christ. This is where the conversation gets interesting.

Chapter 34
God in Three Persons

We struggle with how Mormons can believe in a God who was once a man. To be fair, there is something that we believe about God that Mormons struggle with. So often, the first thing that LDS will ask me about our beliefs is whether or not we believe in the Trinity. When I say yes, typically there are follow-up questions like "How can one thing be three things?" or "When Jesus was praying in the Garden of Gethsemane, who was he praying to, himself?" These questions feel like "gotcha" questions. Our LDS friends do not understand how we can possibly believe that about God.

I explain that we believe in the Trinity because the Bible says that there is one God. Deuteronomy 6:4: "Hear, O Israel: The Lord thy God is one Lord." Then it calls three different persons God. The Father is called God in many places. Romans 1:7: "Grace and peace to you from God our Father." No one doubts the deity of the Father. There are numerous verses where Jesus is called God. Romans 9:5: "Christ, who is God over all, forever praised!" The Holy Spirit is called God in Acts 5:8.

If one is looking for a specific verse where the Trinity is taught, I usually turn to Matthew 28:19: "Therefore, go and make disciples of all nations, baptizing them in the name of the Father and of the Son and of the Holy Spirit."

Grammatically, that does not make sense. It should say baptize them in the "names" of the Father, Son, and Holy Spirit. It says "name." In this critical verse where Jesus commissions the disciples to go and make disciples of all nations, he communicates implicitly that God is not just one but three.

One of the reasons Mormons have such a hard time with the Trinity is because of their belief that God is literally a flesh-and-bone, space, time, and matter being. If that is the case, then I can understand how the Trinity would make no sense. It does not make sense that three different persons could be one person.

That is not the doctrine of the Trinity. When we say that the one true God exists eternally in three persons—Father, Son, and Holy Spirit—we are saying that God is one in being and three in person.

When we say God is one in being, we are talking about "what" God is. We are saying God is infinite, omnipotent, omnipresent, omniscient, and unchangeable. There are three whos—three persons: the Father, Son, and Holy Spirit—that possess those attributes.

There are statements Jesus makes that are difficult to understand. For example, in John 14:28, Jesus says that "the Father is greater than I." How can Jesus be God and the Father be God when Jesus says that the Father is greater than He is?

We need to realize that in Christ, God became one of us by taking upon himself a real body of flesh and bones. Athanasius put it well in the 4th century when he said of Jesus, "He became what He was not. He remained what He was."

Jesus became a man. He remained God. In becoming one of us, Jesus, the Son of God, submitted to the will of the Father. In that sense, the Father was greater than the Son.

That is the whole idea of Philippians 2:6: "Who, being in very nature God, did not consider equality with God something to be grasped, but made Himself nothing, taking the very nature of a servant, being made in human likeness." When you humble yourself and submit to someone else, it does not make you less than that person. In nature, Jesus remained equal to the Father. The Son came to this Earth and submitted Himself to the will of the Father. Jesus obeyed and gave glory to His Father. That did not make Jesus any less God.

When I was a young man, I lived in my father's house. I submitted (quite imperfectly) to my father's will. I was also the kid who would say, "My dad is better than your dad."

Was I any less of a human being for praising my dad? My parents moved to Utah when they were in their late seventies. I was my dad's pastor. He would sit in the front row every Sunday, and after every sermon he would come and say the same thing to me: "That was the best sermon I have ever heard."

Yes, he was just a little bit biased. Did the fact that he praised me make him any less human? Of course not.

The Son came and glorified the Father and submitted to the Father. There is also a time when the Father glorifies the Son. Philippians 2:11: "Therefore God exalted Jesus to the highest place and gave him the name that is above every name. That at the name of Jesus every knee should bow, in Heaven and on Earth and under the Earth, and every tongue confess that Jesus Christ is Lord, to the glory of God the Father." After Jesus ascends into Heaven, there is this moment where the Father directs the praise of the universe to the Son and says let His name be above every name. When the Son is glorified by the Father, does that make the Father any less God?

There is a third member of the Trinity, the Holy Spirit. The Son sends the Holy Spirit into the world. The Holy Spirit does not come into the world to bring glory to Himself. The Holy Spirit brings glory to Christ. Does that make the Holy Spirit any less God? Of course not. This is the way it is with God. The Son glories in the Father and the Father glories in the Son, and the Spirit glorifies the Son and on and on it goes.

Sometimes, in discussing the Trinity, LDS will say to me, "This whole Trinity thing is confusing to me. I can't understand it." From there, the idea is that "if I cannot understand it, then it must not be true."

The fact that I cannot comprehend something does not mean it is not real. God is not like us. I am living in this material body and am bound by space and time. God is not bound by it. He existed before it.

There is something telling about the universe that God created. It is a trinitarian universe. There is one universe that consist of three things: space, time, and matter. Space consists of three things: length, width, and height. Time consists of three things: past, present, and future. Matter consists of three things: solid, liquid, and gas. The universe says something about the God who created it.

We may have a hard time comprehending the Trinity, but that doesn't make it unimportant. Back in the 4th century, when the council of Nicaea was formulating the doctrine of the Trinity, it was noted that what was being disputed was essentially one word.

Athanasius, who stood for the orthodox definition of the Trinity, said that the Father, Son, and the Holy Spirit were of the same substance. The word for same substance is "homoousious." It means that each person of the Trinity—the Father, Son, and Holy Spirit—are God in every way.

The counter position was that of Arius, who said the Father, Son, and Holy Spirit were "homoiousios," which means "similar substance." Arius said that the Father, Son, and Holy Spirit were "like" one another. Athanasius was made to feel that he was quibbling over the addition of one letter of one word.

Athanasius was told that "the whole world was against him." Athanasius replied and said, "Then Athanasius will be against the world."

Athanasius knew that that this one word (and that one *iota* within that word) made all the difference in the world. How so? What if, as Arius taught, Jesus had not always been God, but *became* the Son of God? It would mean that He is a creature and not creator. It would mean that Jesus is the best of us, but He is still essentially a creature.

If He is merely a creature, then Jesus becomes a great example for us to emulate. Our greatest need is not another standard of behavior that we can fall short of. We need a savior. The gospel is that God became one of us in Jesus. Because Jesus is God, He can rescue us from sin and death.

I bring up Athanasius and Arius to highlight the fact that this discussion about the Trinity is nothing new. It has been going on for centuries. The doctrine of the Trinity prevailed in the council of Nicaea because Athanasius was able to make the point that the Trinity was something the church had always believed.

The gospel that we preach is the same one that Jude wrote of when he spoke of "contending for the faith once for all delivered to the saints." Why would we contend for something like the Trinity? We contend for the doctrine of the Trinity because so much depends on it.

There is another idea about God that no one will argue about. It is the simple statement that "God is love." G.K. Chesterton in his book *The Everlasting Man* says that if the Trinity is not a reality, then to say that "God is love" is meaningless.

Chesterton says, "If there be a being without beginning, existing before all things, was He loving when there was nothing to be loved? If through that unthinkable eternity He is lonely, what is the meaning of saying He is love?"

How could God be love if He was alone without anyone to love? The reality of the Trinity is that before the world began, the three persons of the Trinity existed in an infinite relationship of love with one another. Jesus speaks of that love when he prays to the Father in John 17:24 and says, "You loved me before the creation of the world."

The Trinity answers one of the great questions of life. Why did God create us? The answer is in Genesis 2:27: "So God created mankind in His own image, in the image of God He created them; male and female, he created them." The primary way in which we bear the image of God is that God created someone who could experience what God experiences. God is love. We are created with the ability to love and be loved.

That is what life is all about. When Jesus was asked, "Teacher, which is the greatest commandment in the Law?" Jesus replied: "'Love the Lord your God with all your heart and with all your soul and with all your mind.' This is the first and greatest commandment. And the second is like it: 'Love your neighbor as yourself.' All the Law and the Prophets hang on these two commandments." (Matthew 22:36-40)

Jesus tells us that life is all about loving God and loving one another. All of us understand that to be human is to love and be loved. That did not happen by accident. We were created that way by design.

Chapter 35
Pork Chop Theology

We need to understand that the Trinity is an attempt by finite creatures to understand an infinite God. We come to understand the Trinity and believe it by taking into account the whole counsel of scripture. Yes, it seems complicated at times. In reality, God has made it simple for us. Ultimately, God made himself known by becoming one of us.

John 1:18: "No one has ever seen God, but the one and only Son, who is Himself God and is in closest relationship with the Father, has made Him known." He came to be with us in person. We know God through Jesus.

In the conversation between Jesus and the Samaritan woman, Jesus is introducing her to some difficult-to-understand concepts. Jesus is telling her about a brand-new way of looking at the world, and she is having a hard time understanding it. In John 4:25, the woman said, "I know that Messiah (called Christ) is coming. When he comes, he will explain everything to us."

This was this woman's way of saying that there are some things we are never going to be able to figure out. There are things that won't be made clear until the Messiah shows up.

Like the Jews, Samaritans believed that one day God was going to send the Messiah who would right the wrongs in the world and answer all questions. Until then, she is saying, "Let's just agree to disagree."

John 4:26: "Then Jesus declared, 'I, the one speaking to you—I am he.'" Jesus is saying that He is the one both Jew and Samaritan have been looking for.

She does not dismiss his claim. There is something about Jesus and the way He has spoken to the woman that makes her believe Jesus might be who He has claimed to be.

At that same moment, something happens that changes the dynamic of their conversation. John 4:27-30: "Just then His disciples returned and were surprised to find Him talking with a woman. But no one asked, 'What do you want?' or 'Why are you talking with her?'"

This is an awkward moment. Earlier, the Samaritan woman had been surprised when this Jewish rabbi asked her for a drink. Now it is the disciples' turn to be surprised. They cannot conceive of a reason why Jesus would ever talk to a Samaritan woman.

This woman no doubt senses the tension and takes this as an opportunity to be on her way. John 4:28-29: "Then, leaving her water jar, the woman went back to the town and said to the people . . ." As she heads back into town, she leaves her water jar behind at the well. Clearly, she has every intention of returning to get it. After hearing Jesus claim to be the one that both Jews and Samaritans are waiting for, she does not say, "Yeah, right." She goes into town and says to the people there in John 4:29, "Come, see a man who told me everything I ever did."

Look at what has happened here. This woman has gone to the well in the middle of the day to avoid seeing anyone. Now she goes into town and tells everyone she can find to "come and see a man." She has been disappointed by lots of men in her life; now she has met a man that is different. Jesus is so different that she asks John 4:29b-30, "Could this be the Messiah?"

They all knew this woman, and they wondered what had happened to her at the well to give her the courage to come and tell them about the man she met there. "They came out of the town and made their way toward Him." Here is this woman who has been rejected by her people. She had stopped gathering at the well when all the other women gathered together. She no longer belongs. She had become an outsider in her own culture and religion. Now here she was, leading a group of her people out to meet Jesus.

How does that happen? She has met Jesus. After meeting Jesus, she gets involved in the most important work that we could ever be involved in. It is not a commitment to a new religion. She starts bringing people to Jesus. As a result of her witness, people start making their way toward Jesus.

Through the years, I have watched lots of people raised in the LDS Church come to faith in the Christ of the Bible and become a part of the fellowship of CenterPoint Church. Why would anyone make that journey?

One of the things we talk about at CenterPoint is "Pork Chop Theology." The idea came from my favorite dog ever, a Labrador retriever named Bubba. Bubba loved to chew bones. Sometimes as he chewed these dry bones, I would play with him and try to get the bone away from him. Bubba would fight me to keep the dry bone. One way to get him to forget about the bone was to drop a piece of meat (say a pork chop) in front of him.

Religion is like the dry bone. It promises something that it cannot deliver. People will hang onto the dry bone because it is all they have and all they know. They are not going to give up that dry bone without a fight. Traditionally, a lot of ministry to Mormons has been fighting over that dry bone.

Sometimes, Mormons will give up on the dry bone because they have given up hope of ever finding any meat on the bone. What we are trying to do is to give them the pork chop, give them the real deal. The Jesus of the New Testament is the real deal.

The Samaritan woman has just encountered Jesus, and then she does something that is so important. She goes and invites her friends and neighbors to come and meet him. We believe that the place today where people can go and see Jesus is through the body of Christ, the local church. We want our people to do what this woman has done—to meet Jesus, and then to go out and invite their friends to church. We want to create an invitational culture.

As a church, we have attracted newcomers in a lot of different ways. It helps to have a building that is visible on the freeway, but I would still say that more people have come to us through personal invitation than anything else. The building gives us enough credibility that people think it might be worth their while to check it out. Once they come in the doors, we have to realize this culture is all about family. One of the first questions any Mormon asks when they visit CenterPoint for the first time is "could I bring my family members here?" We want to help them answer that question with a resounding "yes."

One of the most important questions we ask as we plan our Sunday services is whether or not what we have planned is something our people would want to invite their family members to. Asking this question influences the way that we talk about all sorts of issues, like giving.

We also try to eliminate what we call "the weird factor." Yes, evangelicals have all sorts of different ways of being weird. Believe me, I have gone through more cringeworthy moments in our church than I like to remember. Mormons are tired of being thought of as weird. They do not want to exchange one form of religious weirdness for another.

That question, "Why would anyone ever leave the LDS Church and become a part of a church like ours?" is one I have had numerous opportunities to answer.

A few years back, Erik and Melanie began to come to CenterPoint. They were, in many ways, a model LDS family. They were both from very devout LDS backgrounds. Erik is a returned missionary and a former bishop.

One day, Erik called me after a conversation he had just had with his parents about where he was in his faith. He told them of his decision to leave the LDS Church. He told them of the new life he had found in Jesus, and that he was attending CenterPoint.

He had high hopes that his family would embrace this change and want to know more. His family did not want to know more. He was not exactly disowned, but clearly, a line was drawn between him and his family. He knew that things would never be the same. He felt a tremendous sense of loss. He called me and said to me, "Scott, tell me that it is worth it."

That was one of those moments where I realized how much was at stake in what we are doing at CenterPoint and how much responsibility churches like ours have in this state. My response to Erik was, "Yes, Jesus is worth it. He will never let you down, and He will never forsake you."

That is part of the answer, but it was not the whole answer. Erik had experienced the loss of family. He wanted to know if the church would become family for him.

Evangelicals love to talk about a personal relationship with Jesus. Yes, it is personal in that no one can decide for me. But that personal relationship with Jesus is not a private relationship. My hopes and prayers are that we will be family to people like Erik and Melanie who have lost family. In the end, I can say that it was worth it.

I also told Erik that the people of CenterPoint will, at some point, disappoint him. Our fellow members in the body of Christ will probably, at some point, hurt us. Sometimes, this thing called the church will break your heart. I went on to say that part of following Jesus is loving what he loves. Jesus loves his church and laid down his life for it, even with all of its problems.

As hard as it is to shepherd sheep, there is nothing more rewarding than leadership in the local church. Erik has stayed and found family and now leads a group in our church that helps people leaving the LDS Church transition to a new faith in Christ.

As I look at evangelicalism in my lifetime, it seems like we are looking for some way to be distinctive, so we think of ways of setting ourselves apart. We wear Christian-themed t-shirts and WWJD bracelets. We try to be distinctive in the way that we worship. You can only be an "on fire Christian" if you raise your hands when you worship, and so on.

Here is what was different about the early church. They clothed themselves with compassion, kindness, gentleness, humility, and patience (Colossians 3:14). They loved one another. What was different about the early church was that people without a lot in common were able to get along because they had Jesus in common. I believe that we have the same opportunity in the church in America today.

Chapter 36
Lift Up Your Eyes

One of the amazing things about Jesus is that He is able to accomplish work in the lives of different people within the same situation. Obviously, He was working in the life of the Samaritan woman. He was also doing something in the lives of his disciples.

While Jesus had been talking with this woman at the well, the disciples were in town buying food. When they returned to the well, they were surprised to see Jesus talking to a Samaritan woman. Jesus was a rabbi, and this was a culture with clear expectations when it came to the conduct of rabbis. They avoided women. They would especially avoid contact with Samaritan women.

The disciples are concerned with how this looks. Jesus is concerned about a woman who has been dying within a religious culture that has not brought her life. The disciples are so bound up in their preconceived ideas about religion that they cannot see what Jesus sees. The disciples respond to this awkward moment by bringing him food.

John 4:31: "Meanwhile his disciples urged him, 'Rabbi, eat something.'" Maybe in addressing him as "rabbi" they are trying to remind him of his role and the expectations of his position. John 4:32: "But he said to them, 'I have food to eat that you know nothing about.'" John 4:33: "Then his disciples said to each other, 'Could someone have brought him food?'"

They have just proven themselves to be as clueless spiritually as this woman had been earlier. This woman had been unable to understand Jesus when He spoke of "living water." Her mind was on drinking water. Here, Jesus is talking about a different kind of food, and the disciples can only think of food that would fill their stomachs.

I can relate to spiritual cluelessness. As I look back at over 30 years of ministry here, I realize there is an awful lot I have been wrong about and many things I have been blind to. Spiritual blindness is not just a Samaritan characteristic. The disciples of Jesus are just as blind to what he is doing.

It is also important to be reminded or who it is telling this story. This is the Apostle John. Most scholars believe John wrote his account of the life of Jesus at the end of his life. As an old man, it was important for him to let everyone know how foolish he and the other apostles had been at times.

One of the things that frightens me about writing this book is that anyone reading it would get the sense that I (Scott McKinney) have it all together. I do not have all of the answers, and neither have I arrived at a place of great insight or perfection. I haven't. I am a flawed and fallen human being. If I have done one thing, it would be that I have kept showing up and pointing people to Jesus.

That is what John does here. He remembers how Jesus responds to the cluelessness of his followers. "'My food,' said Jesus, 'is to do the will of Him who sent me and to finish His work.'" That work is the great work of salvation that Jesus ultimately accomplishes on the cross. The reason Jesus is willing to go to the cross is that Jesus loves people.

By talking to this woman at the well, Jesus is trying to communicate to the disciples that it is not just Jews that matter to God. Everyone matters. For just one moment, He wants them to see what he sees. He says in 4:35, "Don't you have a saying, 'It's still four months until harvest'? I tell you, open your eyes and look at the fields! They are ripe for harvest."

What Jesus is asking them to do is to look at this situation with fresh eyes. He recognizes that it is still four months more until the harvest. It is still spring. But He says lift up your heads and look out at the fields with a different kind of vision. As the disciples lifted up their heads and saw the fields, it seems reasonable to assume that this woman was returning with a group of Samaritan villagers.

The word for "ripe" there is actually the word for "white." My understanding here is that Jesus asks the disciples to look up, and as they do, they see Samaritan villagers wearing white walking through the fields on their way to see Jesus. The fields are filled with a different kind of harvest. It is a harvest of people.

The big takeaway here for our church and churches like ours in Utah is that we have to see what Jesus sees and care about what he cares about. Through the years, there has been all sorts of pressure to care about all kinds of things.

We could focus all of our attention on proving that the LDS Church is not true. We could be the anti-Mormon church. We could become a church where the only thing that matters is winning arguments and being right. The only problem with that is that churches like that attract people that love to argue. It does not take very long for those same people to start turning on one another.

We could be a non-Mormon club. We could make it our goal to gather all of the non-Mormons that have moved here because of work or school and try to make them happy while they are living here. We could try to balance all of the competing ideas of all sorts of "Christians" from all sorts of different backgrounds, all of whom seem to have strong ideas about how church ought to be done. Good luck with that.

We could focus on making our LDS neighbors happy. We could make it our goal to be as inoffensive as possible. We could blur the lines between what we teach and what the LDS Church teaches and become functionally what the LDS Church already thinks we are: The Church of Junior Varsity Christians.

We could get involved in politics and become a political action committee. There are all of these pressures that are brought to bear on the church. Sometimes, the pressures seem so great that it feels crushing. When that pressure is at its greatest, it is important to look to Jesus and to hear what He says and see what He sees. It is important to see that the great work we have been called to is His work of coming to seek and save the lost.

Afterword

John 4:37-38: "Then he said to his disciples, 'The harvest is plentiful, but the workers are few. Ask the Lord of the harvest, therefore, to send out workers into his harvest field.'"

Jesus ends this encounter at Jacob's Well in Samaria by stating that "the harvest is plentiful, but the workers are few." When it comes to the work of Jesus, that always seems to be the case. It is true in the case of this harvest field of Utah. I do believe that the harvest is plentiful in Utah.

I have written this book in the hope that it would be an encouragement to the workers already here in this harvest field and that it might inspire others to come and be part of what God is doing in this place.

Over the last 30 plus years, I have seen a huge change. Early on, it did not seem there was a lot of harvesting going on. That is the way it works with farming. It takes time. You break the hard ground, and then you sow the seed. Then you watch over the fields as the plants grow. You protect the plants from disease and insects. Finally, it is harvest time. You gather the fruit in.

One of the things I can say about this whole process is that along the way, there never seemed to be enough resources and people to gather the harvest. We cannot wait until we have those resources to begin to work. All we can do is show up and then keep on showing up. As we work, we continue to pray that the Lord of the harvest will continue to send workers into the harvest.

Afterword

The amazing thing about any harvest is that the seeds of future growth are in the fruit. The thing that gets me excited about the future of a lot of local churches like ours in Utah is that people from this place and culture are coming to faith in Jesus and staying here to be part of the harvest. I am convinced there is a genuine hunger for Jesus in LDS culture. If there is one thing I hope for, it is that as more and more people from an LDS background find Jesus, more and more will stay and be part of the harvest.

It is also good to see that Jesus is sending workers into this field from other places. In my journey here in Utah thirty years ago, people would say, "Utah? Why would you want to live there?" Today, there are lots of people moving here for work, and Utah has one of the best economies in the country.

There are tremendous educational opportunities here. We live in a beautiful valley where there is a low crime rate along with a kid-friendly environment. Our hope is that as people move here, they will see their need for Jesus and in time lift up their eyes and gain a sense of spiritual purpose here. One of the things we can never underestimate is the impact people have when they seek to follow Jesus where they work and live.

Jesus followers cannot live isolated and alone. We need one another. There is a need for healthy, lifegiving churches in Utah. I am excited to see pastors moving here to plant churches. As a church, CenterPoint wants to do everything we can to encourage the growth of healthy churches here in Utah. That is why this book was written.

To those who are here and to those who are on their way, let me end with a verse God has used as an encouragement through the years. 1 Corinthians 15:58: "Therefore, my dear brothers and sisters, stand firm. Let nothing move you. Always give yourselves fully to the work of the Lord, because you know that your labor in the Lord is not in vain."

Being involved in the work that Jesus is doing is not easy. So much of life is finding something worth doing, and then to keep showing up to do those things that matter. That is true in our families and our relationships. It is true of the work of the local church. The things that matter never seem to be easy. They are worth it.

About the Author

Scott McKinney has been the pastor of the church known today as CenterPoint since 1989.

Scott received a B.A. in History from Cal State San Bernardino in 1976. In 1980, he received a Masters of Divinity from the Talbot School of Theology at Biola University. After that, he was a school administrator and football coach at Capistrano Valley Christian School in San Juan Capistrano, California, for seven years—followed by three years as an associate pastor at Cypress Evangelical Free Church in Cypress, California. Scott has been married to his wife, Sara, since 1979. Together, they have four children and fifteen grandchildren.

Since arriving in this valley, the McKinneys have sought to do more than lead a church. They have been a part of the community and have sought to be a blessing to it. In turn, they have come to realize that, in living here, they have received much more than they have given. They are grateful to have been able to spend their lives and raise their children in this place they call home.

Made in the USA
Monee, IL
03 November 2021